FENG SHUI

FENG SHUI

STEPHEN SKINNER

PARRAGON

ACKNOWLEDGEMENTS

To Lillian Too who suggested that I take up pen again and write another feng-shui book
exactly 20 years after I completed my first, the *Living Earth Manual of Feng-shui*.

First published in Great Britain in 1997 by
Parragon
Queen Street House
4-5 Queen Street
Bath BA1 1HE

ISBN: 0-7525-2385-6

Produced by Haldane Mason, London

Acknowledgements
Art Director: Ron Samuels
Editor: Jo-Anne Cox
Designer: Zoë Mellors
Illustrator: Stephen Dew
Picture Research: Jo-Anne Cox
Indexer: Lydia Darbyshire

Printed in Italy

Picture acknowledgements
All photographs by Joff Lee with the exception of the following:
Ace Photo Agency: 67 (top); **Heather Angel:** 90 (bottom);
Greg Evans International: 27; **Sydney Francis:** 88;
The Garden Picture Library: 74, 76, 78, 79, 80, 87 (both), 91, 92;
Sally & Richard Greenhill: 38, 56, 66 (bottom);
The Image Bank: 13, 14, 29 (top), 29 (bottom right), 29 (bottom left), 29 (centre left),
32 (left), 32 (centre), 32 (right), 32 (far right), 48, 67 (bottom), 83;
London Aerial Photo Library: 17; **Rex Features Ltd:** 6, 7, 15, 29 (centre right), 32 (far left);
Stephen Skinner: 46 (bottom left); **Trip Photographic Library:** 22 (both), 58;
Michael Tse: 10; **Elizabeth Whiting & Associates:** 68, 70, 72;
Zefa Pictures: 29 (main, left), 29 (main, right), 85

Every effort has been made to trace the copyright holders and we apologize in advance for any
unintentional omissions. We would be pleased to insert the appropriate acknowledgement
in any subsequent edition of this publication.

The materials which appear on pages 64 (top right), 90 (top right) and 93 (top) were supplied by
The Feng Shui Company, Ballard House, 37 Norway Street, London SE10 9DD (07000 781901).

contents

Note: *Remember that in all traditional feng-shui illustrations (in line with Chinese practice) South is always shown at the top of the page and North at the bottom of the page. However North still means the direction North, even in the Southern Hemisphere. Feng-shui practitioners in Australia, for example, should not reverse these directions simply because of the different hemisphere.*

INTRODUCTION

Rich & Famous Devotees of Feng-shui

Feng-shui (pronounced 'foong-shway') is the ancient Chinese art of harnessing the heavens and the earth to bring health, wealth and good fortune, by tuning in to the environment, seasonal changes, tides and vibrations of nature.

Richard Branson, one of the many successful business people who increasingly look to feng-shui to give them an extra edge.

The principles of feng-shui are designed to alter your environment, your home and your heart, so that you feel at peace with yourself and the universe, and therefore able to use those changes in the tides of fortune that ceaselessly churn through your life to your best advantage.

Famous believers

The practice of feng-shui dates back thousands of years but it is still used today by many of the rich and famous who would not give it a second glance if they thought it was simply an ancient superstition. Even one of the most successful banks in the world today, the HSBC Group which owns the Midland Bank and has gone from strength to strength, had its head offices designed with advice from a feng-shui practitioner.

Lillian Too, the ex-managing director of the Grindlays Dao Heng bank in Hong Kong and the former deputy chairman of the billion dollar company that owns Harvey Nichols, not only believes implicitly in feng-shui but is the best known writer on the subject.

Donald Trump and Richard Branson have both used the services of feng-shui practitioners and look how successful they are! Another convert is Anita Roddick whose Body Shop chain uses feng-shui principles in its store design. Boy George, too, has been a long time believer in feng-shui and attributes much of his success to its beneficial practices.

Feng-shui in the business world

In the early 1990s the Credit Lyonnais bank produced a light-hearted Feng-shui Stock Market Index designed to predict the moves of the *Hang Seng* Index (the Hong Kong Stock Market). In December 1992 the Asian *Wall Street Journal* ran an article on the Feng-shui Index confirming that it had predicted the major turning points of the *Hang Seng* over the previous 12 months. The bank has commissioned similar indexes every year since. Although feng-shui does not claim to predict stock market moves, the uncanny accuracy of these predictions certainly made people more aware of feng-shui.

It is no coincidence that in Hong Kong and Taiwan many of the buildings have feng-shui inspired features, and that these two states have amongst the highest per capita income in the world, closely followed in Asia by Singapore and Malaysia, two other advanced 'tiger' economies. Businessmen in these countries take feng-shui very seriously.

Anyone familiar with the tycoons of the Far East will know that many of them regularly consult feng-shui masters in the course of their business, especially where it concerns property. It is well known for example that the owners of the Hyatt Hotel in Singapore have successfully used feng-shui advice to help increase their trade.

Major UK real estate agents, such as Hamptons, use feng-shui practitioners to check that new developments will sell to an increasingly choosy clientele. Developers like Wimpey homes have gone as far as producing a beginner's guide to 'Feng Shui in your Home' which is issued to all of its new home buyers. In addition, the *Daily Mail* newspaper now runs a regular weekly page on feng-shui.

Feng-shui: the past and future

In the past the practice of feng-shui was limited to the Emperor of China and his family and functionaries. Ordinary people practised it on pain of death. However, you don't have to be an international bank, a huge corporation or a famous rock star to use feng-shui. And you don't need to generate the enormous amounts of good fortune that is required to make a multi-billion international company successful. This book will explain how even small changes in the feng-shui environment of your home can bring worthwhile benefits to the health, luck and happiness sectors of your life.

Don't expect feng-shui to help you win the lottery: it simply doesn't work like that. Feng-shui is not magic, but a natural practice. Practised correctly it will slowly but surely increase your feeling of rightness with the world, contentment will quickly replace dissatisfaction. Things which used to irritate you will lose their sting and gradually you will waste less time on unproductive actions or swimming fruitlessly against the unrepenting tide of life. Increasingly you will instinctively spend more time on things that bring you happiness and better fortune.

Despite wildly fluctuating fortunes, Donald Trump is reputed to be interested in feng-shui.

Wind & Water

In Chinese *feng* means wind and *shui* means water. If you look up to heaven and then down to the surface of the earth, what you are likely to see in between are clouds: these clouds consist of wind and water. The ancient Chinese saw wind and water as the intermediaries between heaven and earth. They thought that heaven directly affected their progress through life in a much more fundamental way than by simply providing changeable weather.

It is clear that at the very least water is the sustainer of all life, whether plant, animal or human. Likewise, it is the wind which carries water from place to place, causes evaporation from the sea, and enables rain to fall on what would otherwise be parched land. Wind and water are therefore essential to our survival.

In addition, for a feng-shui practitioner these elements also carry the invisible life energy force *ch'i*. Therefore to ensure that there is an abundance of *ch'i* in a site or a home, it is important to observe the flow of wind and water and their interaction with the land.

The effects of ch'i

Ch'i acts on every level – on the human level it is the energy flowing through the acupuncture meridians or channels of the body (see pages 10-11); at the agricultural level it is the force which, if not stagnant, ensures fertile crops; and at the climatic level it is the energy carried on the wind and by the waters.

The mapping of these *ch'i* flows, and their deflection or enhancement are the main principles of feng-shui. In other words, after mapping these

We live immersed in air, whose changing tides are the winds. Gentle breezes bring contentment while strong winds disperse life-enhancing ch'i.

ch'i flows, it is often necessary to correct, enhance or deflect them. For example, feng-shui practitioners maintain that just placing a small mirror or a wind-chime precisely in the correct place can sometimes make an enormous difference to your life. Instead of finding yourself always battling against life and your surroundings, whether in your love life or your career, you will find with the correct placement of some almost insignificant feng-shui 'cure' that suddenly everything seems to go your way. The most unexpected meetings develop into major and profitable business relationships, or precipitate a significant career advancement. Partners and colleagues suddenly seem more helpful, and you feel more in control of your life.

Accepting feng-shui

It is not easy to see why the placement of a mirror or even a change in the position of your bed should suddenly improve your relationships, but as you read through this book, you will begin to understand and to start experimenting with the simpler methods of feng-shui. The proof of the pudding will be in the eating! You don't have to believe in feng-shui for it to work for you, any more than you have to believe in aspirin for it to cure your headache.

Don't think of feng-shui as thinking superstitiously, but rather as thinking symbolically. Famous psychologists such as Carl Jung proved that the subconscious is impressed by symbols which the conscious mind might see as trivial. Although feng-shui actually works because of concentrations and dispersals of *ch'i*, if you find this difficult to accept you can always justify your feng-shui successes by reasoning that you have impressed your subconscious sufficiently for it to work on your behalf towards your desired ends. You could then consider the practices of feng-shui simply a shorthand set of rules for impressing your subconscious. Either way, it does not really matter, because the simple fact is that feng-shui really works.

Don't however make the mistake of thinking that feng-shui is arbitrary. You cannot just make up the rules as you go along. Sloppy and incorrect use of feng-shui can be just as effective in destroying your luck, as correct use can be in building it up.

The changing nature of flowing water not only symbolizes the theory behind feng-shui, but is actually one of the agents that carry the life-giving ch'i.

Ch'i: its Sources & Effects

Ch'i is loosely referred to as 'cosmic breath' or 'life force', or more picturesquely the 'dragon's breath'. *Ch'i* flows through the human body and only departs on death, after which the body disintegrates. *Ch'i* is therefore literally 'the breath of life'.

Although not charted by Western medicine methods, acupuncture practitioners have long known of the existence of *ch'i*, and have built up elaborate maps of the 'meridians' or channels it uses to flow through the body. Acupuncture has been used to cure a number of medical conditions. Although acupuncture is widely accepted in the West as a valid form of therapy, there is still some progress to be made before the circulation of *ch'i* energy through the human body is accepted by Western science as an explanation of acupuncture.

Ch'i and martial arts

Further concrete proof of the existence of *ch'i* is afforded by martial arts techniques which display extraordinary speed, strength and

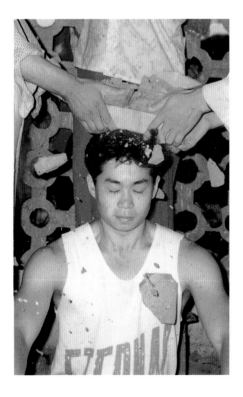

The ability of the human body to perform almost superhuman feats, such as breaking bricks over the head, is increased by the accumulation of ch'i *in the body.*

agility, and which are attributed by their practitioners to a concentration of *ch'i* in their body. Kung Fu masters believe that *ch'i* can be concentrated in the body, allowing the body to perform almost supernatural feats, such as breaking concrete blocks with the edge of a hand. With the correct breathing techniques, in other words with the correct concentration of *feng* or air, the Kung Fu master gives his body a strength and imperviousness to injury that would otherwise be impossible.

Ch'i in the land

Ch'i also flows through and enlivens the earth as well as the body. For example, slow meandering rivers or streams accumulate *ch'i* in the land according to feng-shui masters. This accumulation of *ch'i* both strengthens the body and the land. In short, through *feng* (wind or air) and *shui* (water) we can accumulate *ch'i*, which is beneficial to both man and his environment.

Accumulating ch'i

Those adept with the methods of internal alchemy or the martial arts have learned to accumulate *ch'i* in the body by a hard and exhausting regime, but for most of us the degree of passive absorption of *ch'i* from our surroundings, either at home or work, is the chief factor governing our energy and lucidity level. An increase of *ch'i* in a site automatically benefits those living there, and feng-shui provides methods for doing this.

Living near or on concentrations of *ch'i* is reputed to be a source of greater concentration and clear headedness, abundant wealth, health and happiness. The Chinese see this as an accumulation of 'luck'. Luck, for the Chinese, is not something that just happens, it is something that can be worked at and consciously increased.

This brings us to the basic rules of *ch'i* accumulation, and hence also the basis of feng-shui. Straight lines or fast flowing streams or roads deplete and disperse *ch'i*, leading to the evaporation of luck. Stagnation contributes to the breakdown of *ch'i*, just as *ch'i* disperses when a body dies. The ideal conditions for accumulating *ch'i* are the slow, coiling, sinuous flow of water or wind which accumulate healthy *ch'i* in a suitably protected haven. This *ch'i* must be protected in order to accumulate, but it must also have access to another vigorous flow of *ch'i*, allowing the site to 'tap into a dragon vein', drawing off and hoarding *ch'i* successfully.

The rest of this book will look at how you can, with a bit of ingenuity, modify your home or your office in order to attract and concentrate as much beneficial *ch'i* as possible. If you are buying a new home then these rules may help you select a house or flat where you will be happier and more secure than if you had just purchased the first property that looked like good value.

A typical acupuncture chart, showing the flow of ch'i through the human body, to be found in practitioners' rooms across the world.

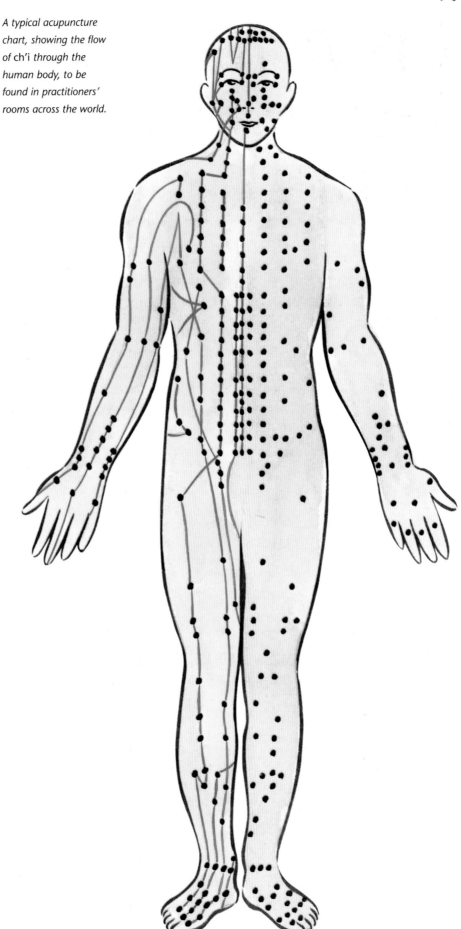

The circulation of ch'i around the human body as conceived by some Taoist schools.

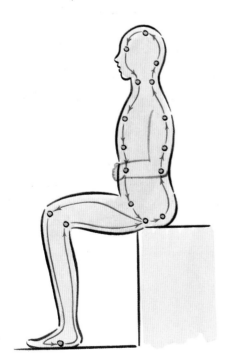

Ch'i 氣 in the Earth

At the very least the Chinese philosophers who considered *feng* (wind or air) and *shui* (water) to be the sustainers of mankind were good geographers and ecologists. However, they took their thinking much further. They understood that wind and water were not the only 'elements' flowing through the landscape and sustaining man. They perceived a more subtle energy flowing through the earth, and they called it *ch'i* or 'cosmic breath'.

CH'I FLOWS IN THE LAND

A classically good feng-shui site, nestled between two mountain ranges, with the ch'i *flows concentrated in the most sheltered part.*

The essence of feng-shui is to analyse a landscape, a town or a house to determine where the most favourable flows of *ch'i* are located, and how to produce new or enhance existing *ch'i* concentrations. The picturesque phrase for this is tapping the 'veins of the dragon'.

Wherever the 'cosmic breath' does not flow freely, stagnant *ch'i* will accumulate. However on the other hand, *ch'i* must not be dispersed or buffeted by rough winds, for unprotected sites are unsuitable for the accumulation of *ch'i*. Naturally meandering watercourses halt and accumulate *ch'i*, but fast flowing streams or those with long straight stretches cannot hold and accumulate their *ch'i* content.

The effects of good *ch'i*

Benign 'cosmic breath' is called *sheng ch'i*, and it brings with it well-being and a feeling of 'everything is right with the world'. Depleted stagnant 'cosmic breath' is called *sha ch'i*. Once your accumulating *ch'i* provides you with an increasingly positive attitude to the world, then it is just a short leap of imagination to see that your reaction to those around you is going to be more positive. Your loved ones will notice it first, then your colleagues at work and finally the world at large. This positive outlook will automatically result in an improvement in your relationships, your work, and as your boss begins to notice, your career prospects. These factors all serve to contribute to what seems to be an increase in luck, followed by an increase in prosperity.

Detecting good and bad *ch'i*

A real feng-shui master will be able to sense the flows of *ch'i* in a site. For the rest of us, the flow of *ch'i* has to be deduced

Water never flows naturally in a straight line. Here the meandering river has folded back on itself. A house positioned correctly in relation to this river (see page 21) will enjoy beneficial ch'i.

from rules or from signs. In a rural setting, animals will often follow lines of *ch'i* flow, and so sometimes paths worn by the tread of animals will trace out the lines of *ch'i*. In cities the flow of *ch'i* is often buffeted or contained by roads and man-made objects. Where these form sharp bends or straight paths, such as motorways or long stretches of telegraph poles, so the *ch'i* flows too rapidly and dangerously. However, those roads which curve, those lined by houses that do not confront each other and gardens which are planted according to feng-shui principles (see chapter 8) accumulate *ch'i* to the benefit of the occupants.

ONE STEP AT A TIME

Feng-shui does not imply a lack of free will, it simply suggests that it is much easier to go with the flow rather than constantly struggle upstream against it. By careful manipulation of feng-shui techniques you can ensure that the flow is going your way. I say careful manipulation because it is necessary to progress slowly with feng-shui by changing a few or even a single arrangement at a time, then allowing things to settle down for a week or so until you can judge whether things have improved as you planned.

If you rush into the deep end and make lots of immediate changes in your surroundings after reading this book, then you will never know for sure which changes have been beneficial and which have not. Worse than that, as a beginner you might make changes which have the reverse effect to the one desired and find that these cancel out the beneficial changes. Feng-shui is in some respects a lot more complex than it first appears.

Lastly, by all means work carefully on your own feng-shui environment, but don't offer to change the feng-shui environment of friends, even with the best of intentions. Unless you are a fully trained feng-shui master or *hsein sheng*, let others make their own mistakes, rather than finding yourself responsible for some major reversal of their fortunes.

Energy Lines:

Avoiding 'Secret Arrows' & *Sha*

Everyone has days when nothing appears to go right, when it does not matter what you do, the results still turn out badly. A build-up in *sha ch'i* has the same effect, and brings with it lost opportunities, legal disputes and other misfortunes. Under such conditions it is impossible to make plans, or get your head 'above water' long enough to get out of the mess.

The long, straight road brings sha ch'i *rushing towards you, while the Eiffel Tower generates 'secret arrows'.*

Sha ch'i or 'killing breath' occurs when the *ch'i* flow is either stagnant or channelled in straight lines which become increasingly destructive forms of energy. *Ch'i* is similar to water in the same way as a gently flowing river is beneficial to transport and agriculture, while a raging torrent or a flash flood is detrimental and sometimes deadly.

Ch'i flowing rapidly in straight lines is particularly dangerous. Modern cities are full of straight lines and therefore generate a lot of *sha ch'i*. It wasn't always so: most medieval European and pre-colonial Asian cities avoid the square grid street plans of modern city planners.

Sources of *sha* and 'secret arrows'

'Secret arrows' are straight lines which by virtue of their power to conduct *sha ch'i* pierce any accumulations of good *ch'i* and reduce their benefit. These lines can be formed by straight ridges, a row of roof-tops, railway embankments, telegraph wires or any set of parallel straight lines, and wherever these lines are directed or converge is subject to the evil influence of these 'secret arrows'. Other examples of such 'secret arrows' include long straight roads leading directly away from the front door of a house, a row of electricity pylons, the pointed edges of large buildings, an overhead beam or a motorway flyover. Such 'secret arrows' can be effectively blocked off from a site or property by a wall, a row of trees or an embankment, or alternatively the 'secret arrows' may be deflected by the correct positioning of mirrors.

A church spire directly aligned with the front door would be another potential source of *sha ch'i*, and it is for this reason that some early Christian missionaries sent to China found hefty opposition to the erection of church buildings by the local population. Rather more modern generators of *sha ch'i* are

satellite dishes which point in the direction of your house, or indeed any sharp and/or shiny surfaces.

'Secret arrows' can be generated externally and be visible through a window or open door, or on a smaller scale they can form as a result of bad furniture placement within a room. Hence a priority with any feng-shui diagnosis is to check for any obvious 'secret arrows' and to establish whether they strike into your bedroom, at your office desk, your dining room or any area where you habitually spend significant amounts of time. In addition you should also open your front door, and standing on the threshold, check for any visible signs of poisonous 'secret arrows'.

These 'secret arrows' tend to destroy one's best efforts. They need to be blocked, deflected or with the use of a mirror reflected back to the source they came from. At the very least such lines should not focus on the places where you normally sleep, work or eat. The elimination of 'secret arrows' takes precedence over any other feng-shui practice, and should be attended to foremost.

Blocking 'secret arrows'

The usual feng-shui 'cure' is to block out the offending sight. If the 'secret arrow' is aimed at the front door of your home, a particularly vulnerable spot, then try blocking the alignment with a hedge or try moving the entrance gate to the front garden to the left or right. If this is not practical, then hang a Pa Kua mirror over the door to relect the 'secret arrows' back to where they came from. The Pa Kua mirror is simply a circular mirror surrounded by eight Trigrams, which is readily available in many Chinese supermarkets, and which will be explained in a later chapter (see pages 88-89).

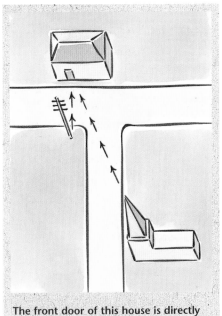

The front door of this house is directly threatened by the 'secret arrows' generated by the telegraph pole and obliquely damaged by the church spire. Such alignments are mainly damaging to front doors, although windows can also be threatened.

Street Placement

Although many of the classical feng-shui texts tend to analyse rural situations where rivers and mountains are the most important landforms, these same principles can also be applied to urban landscapes.

Streets may be treated a little like rivers, although most steets form *sha*-generating straight lines. Tall buildings take the place of mountains. For example in a flat city it is important to have the rear of any site positioned to the North backed by a range of tall buildings.

Classical European examples of long straight streets which generate 'secret arrows' include the long avenues of Paris, many of which fortunately terminate in nothing more vulnerable than commemorative arches rather than some home or public building.

A notable British example of the effect of 'secret arrows' is the Mall, the straight avenue leading up to Buckingham Palace. In the past it ended in a roundabout in front of the Palace gates and all was well because the *sha ch'i* was deflected around the roundabout and away from the Palace gates. Several years ago, however, the roundabout was partially pedestrianised, causing the statue in the middle of the roundabout to become effectively part of the Palace's forecourt. This limited its ability to deflect the 'secret arrows' generated by the Mall. It is perhaps no coincidence to point out that since

that time the popularity of the British monarchy has been dogged by scandal and the very public breakup of the marriages of all the Queen's children, especially that of Charles and Diana. Conversely the residence of the Queen Mother, who retains her public popularity, is set well back from the Mall and is well protected in a feng-shui sense.

Causes of 'secret arrows'

Roundabouts as a whole are a mixed blessing. They do help to 'tame' the stretches of a straight street and deflect 'secret arrows', but for those buildings actually situated around the roundabout, the rapid passage of traffic past them provides little opportunity for the accumulation of gentle *ch'i*. On the whole, streets with heavy traffic produce more *sha ch'i* than streets with light or only occasional traffic.

If possible, you should avoid buying or living in houses directly opposite a road junction, especially one in which a vehicle travelling along one of the roads might, if it did not brake or turn adequately, finish up in your property. Such sites are continually bombarded by *sha ch'i*. Likewise those sites which are irregularly shaped or tightly 'squeezed' between two roads, particularly at a V- or Y-shaped junction, should definitely be avoided.

'Sharp' bridges, viaducts and overhead train lines also produce cutting *ch'i* and are therefore undesirable neighbours. In each of these cases *ch'i* rushing at the house, especially if accelerated by traffic flow, makes the fortunes of the occupants unreliable. However, a road 'cradling' your house, so that you are on the inside of a bend, is beneficial.

Cul-de-sacs are on the whole good for their residents as they act as a *ch'i*-collecting bywater. However, the house or houses directly at the end of the cul-de-sac will suffer the cutting *ch'i* of the full length of the cul-de-sac.

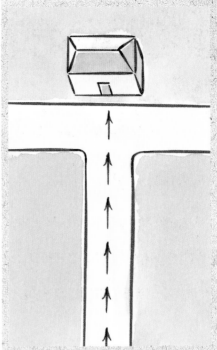

A classic case of a road-generated 'secret arrow'. Try not to buy a house situated at the top of a T-junction, or in a position where a long, straight road 'strikes' the front door.

The house directly at the end of a straight cul-de-sac will be affected by 'secret arrows'. The other houses will, however, benefit from the pooling of *ch'i* at the end of the cul-de-sac.

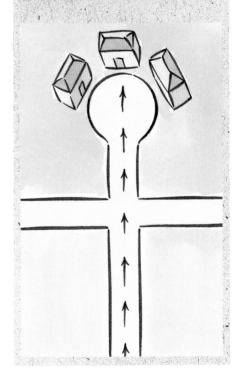

New towns are sometimes sympathetically planned with curving streets which add to the quality of life of their occupants as well as calming traffic speeds. However, on the whole the cutting angles of straight new streets usually destroys local *ch'i* accumulations. In Hong Kong, after a number of expensive legal cases over the disruption of feng-shui caused by new developments, the government decided to hire its own feng-shui experts to advise them whenever they are designing a new development in order to minimize disruption.

Flyovers are an inevitable part of modern life. Unfortunately buildings adjacent to such structures and which

The Ark building in Hammersmith, West London is 'squeezed' in the 'V' between the railway in the foreground and the elevated flyover just behind it, which also 'cuts' it. The large Novotel building behind it also overwhelms its feng-shui.

look as if they are about to be sliced by the flyover will suffer from bad feng-shui. Several buildings adjacent to the M40 elevated motorway where it cuts into the Northwest corner of London have been empty for years. Likewise the 'Ark' building at Hammersmith in West London, which is situated level with a flyover, remained unlet for a number of years after it was first built despite its high-tech construction which won a number of architectural awards.

*The five types of Weather
ch'i extend between
Heaven ch'i and Earth ch'i.*

Earth, Atmosphere & Heaven *Ch'i*

The Chinese believe that there are three kinds of luck: the luck you make yourself (*ren choy*); the gifts that are bestowed upon you by heaven at birth (*t'ien choy*); and the benefits that come from your environment or 'earth luck' (*ti choy*). You cannot easily affect your 'heaven luck', but you can affect your 'earth luck'.

The ridges and lines in the landscape form the body, veins and pulse of the Earth 'dragon' whilst streams, pools and underground watercourses are thought to be the dragon's blood. The veins and watercourses both carry *ch'i*, the life-force in the earth. Of course, as we discovered in chapter 1, lines of trees, roads and even railways carry or disperse *ch'i* across the landscape. The geometry of the flow of *ch'i* can be amazingly complex, forming a lattice or a network between the main 'dragon veins', for no part of the earth is dead. Some parts are barren and some are stagnant, but none are totally dead.

In this book we are concerned with the laws that govern *ti choy* 'earth luck'. How you take advantage of that luck (*ren choy*) is up to you. *Ch'i* pervades both Heaven and Earth and the space in between, so *ch'i* is divided into:

Earth *ch'i* (*ti ch'i*) or host *ch'i*
This is contained in the 'dragon veins' of the earth. It runs through the earth and along its watercourses and is subject to decay. It is governed by the Later Heaven Sequence of the Trigrams (see pages 34-35).

Heaven *ch'i* (*t'ien ch'i*) or guest *ch'i*
This is affected by the heavens and may overrule the effect of Earth *ch'i*. It is governed by the Earlier Heaven Sequence of Trigrams (see page 35).

Weather *ch'i*
There are five types of weather *ch'i* which mediate between Earth and Heaven *ch'i* in much the same way that man is midway between Heaven and Earth and has some small say in influencing both. The five weather *ch'i* are carried in the rain, sunshine, heat, cold and wind. These are the moveable *ch'i*, the fluctuating elements distributed between the more fixed *ch'i* of Heaven and Earth, and they are a mixture of the nature of both Heaven and Earth. They are subject to decay like the Earth *ch'i*.

A stylized view of the five-clawed Imperial dragon.

Ideal feng-shui conditions

The essence of good feng-shui is to trap the *ch'i* energy flowing through the site and accumulate it without allowing it to go stagnant. The second consideration is to ensure that the *ch'i* is not dispersed.

One of the feng-shui classics, *Han Lung Ching*, says that *ch'i* rides the winds and disperses, meaning that windy, unprotected sites will lose any accumulated *ch'i*. However, when bounded by slow-flowing water the *ch'i* actually halts. Here again are the two elements of feng-shui, wind and water. The wind if tamed to a gentle breeze will bring with it the circulating *ch'i*, while if the water follows a curved pattern and is appropriately oriented it will keep the *ch'i* in the site thereby increasing its physical and spiritual fertility.

The third consideration is not to allow the *ch'i* to become torpid or stagnant in which case it becomes *ssu ch'i* or stagnant *ch'i*. If the site is completely hemmed in so that the air does not circulate or the water nearby is sluggish and stagnant, the ground literally gives off damp and stinking exhalations (*sha*), rendering the place unfit from a feng-shui point of view. *Sha* is the antithesis of *ch'i* and can be translated as 'noxious vapour'. It is sometimes called *sha ch'i* or *feng sha* (noxious wind).

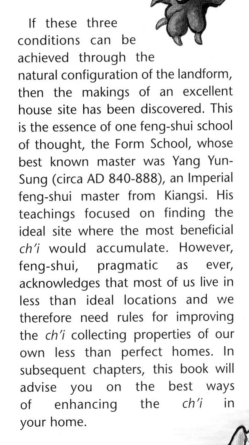

If these three conditions can be achieved through the natural configuration of the landform, then the makings of an excellent house site has been discovered. This is the essence of one feng-shui school of thought, the Form School, whose best known master was Yang Yun-Sung (circa AD 840-888), an Imperial feng-shui master from Kiangsi. His teachings focused on finding the ideal site where the most beneficial *ch'i* would accumulate. However, feng-shui, pragmatic as ever, acknowledges that most of us live in less than ideal locations and we therefore need rules for improving the *ch'i* collecting properties of our own less than perfect homes. In subsequent chapters, this book will advise you on the best ways of enhancing the *ch'i* in your home.

The feng-shui expert looks for the dragon hidden in the landscape.

FENG-SHUI

The Living Water of Rivers

If the watercourses near a property or site run straight and rapidly, the *ch'i* is scattered and wasted before it can serve any beneficial purpose. Those places where the *ch'i* is enclosed to the right and left and has a drainage system carrying off the water in a sinuous course are the best for accumulating *ch'i*.

Chinese dragons were considered to be water creatures, living in rivers or clouds, and not fire-breathing monsters like Western dragons.

Quite often even when defence is not the objective, a Chinese hydraulic engineer will surround a dwelling or village with a curved moat which is open on the south side to receive beneficial *ch'i*. Such diversions of the natural flow of streams show up in dozens of large-scale ordnance survey maps of areas long under Chinese settlement.

Charting *ch'i*

Watercourses are the most obvious flowlines of *ch'i*. In fact the Chinese word for stream actually sounds like *ch'i*. The general rule is that water that flows too quickly or in straight lines conducts *ch'i* away from a spot rapidly, and is therefore undesirable; and that slow, sinuous, deep watercourses, on the other hand, are conducive to the accumulation of *ch'i* especially if they form a pool in front of the property under consideration.

In an urban environment we have to interpret roads in the same light as streams, but with the proviso that as most roads are straight they are more likely to produce damaging 'secret arrows' rather than healthy *ch'i*. Ideally in an urban environment a secret garden containing a pond and stream hidden away behind a high wall is most likely to accumulate beneficial *ch'i*, more so than any meandering road.

Aiding *ch'i*

The landscape can be significantly altered by man to improve feng-shui. Man-made bends can be put in straight river stretches or sharp bends can be made more rounded. Even artificial confluences of rivers or streams can be created. Preferably the house should be nestled amongst tributaries of the river rather than directly on the main or trunk watercourse, especially if the main watercourse runs too fast to accumulate *ch'i*. The more tributaries in the stream, the more potent the *ch'i* accumulation.

A stream flowing from the East or the West is auspicious if it flows directly towards the house, deflects around it, and then meanders away. This is because the *ch'i* brought by the stream enters the house directly (by the straight stretch of water) but is taken away from the house indirectly: it therefore accumulates. If possible the stream leaving the site should be out of sight of the house, so that there is no visible loss of the *ch'i* accumulated.

POSITIVE RIVER LOCATIONS

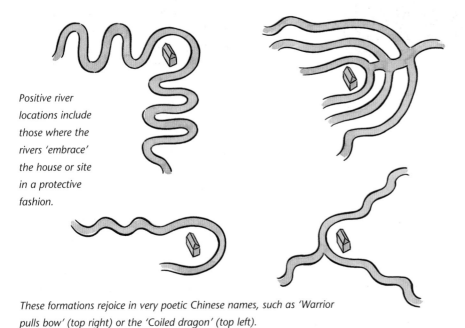

Positive river locations include those where the rivers 'embrace' the house or site in a protective fashion.

These formations rejoice in very poetic Chinese names, such as 'Warrior pulls bow' (top right) or the 'Coiled dragon' (top left).

NEGATIVE RIVER LOCATIONS

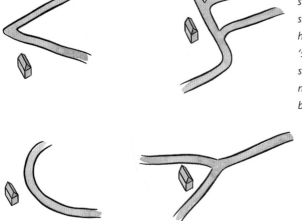

Sharp bends, straight river stretches and houses or sites 'squeezed' in a sharp V or Y do not accumulate beneficial ch'i.

RIVER PATTERNS & SITES

Various real and fantastic river patterns: the more complex patterns were sometimes artificially created by Chinese hydraulic engineers. The red dot shows a potential ch'i accumulating site for a house.

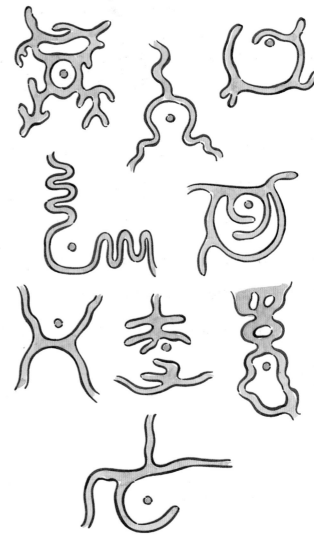

Dragon points

As a curved and meandering course is the best indication of *ch'i*, so the junction of two watercourses is a key dragon point. If the feng-shui practitioner is using a compass, this junction will be a significant and easily aligned siting point.

The junction should form a graceful curve rather than a harsh bend and the watercourse formed should harmoniously cross and re-cross the area in front of the property to enhance positive flows of *ch'i*.

Stream confluences are beneficial because of the concentration of *ch'i*, whilst the branching of a stream flowing through coarse sediment or at the delta of a river is dispersive of *ch'i*. Sharp bends, like straight lines, are unfavourable as they act like 'secret arrows' destroying or removing the *ch'i* accumulations. Curves in the watercourse are much more conductive as they mimic the naturally sinuous shape of a 'dragon'.

Wind or *feng* distributes the water vapour as clouds, which taking the form of dragons in the air, consolidate finally to precipitate life-giving rain on to mountains which, to complete the cycle, are the traditional lair of these dragons. Thus the elements wind and water, which are of course the essence of feng-shui, act through dragons, effecting the earth and the life upon it.

Mountains & Dragon Bones

Symbolically, the landscape betrays the presence of *ch'i* in its shape. To an advanced practitioner of feng-shui the flows of *ch'i* beneath the surface of the landscape are as obvious as the *ch'i* flow strength or weakness detected in the body by an acupuncturist.

The extraordinary mountains of southern China, where the five Element types of mountains are easily picked out.

C*h'i* is symbolized in its positive (Yang) form as a dragon, and in its negative (Yin) form as a tiger. The two different *ch'i* currents in the earth's crust, the one male (positive), the other female (negative), are called, respectively, the green dragon and the white tiger. Looking South, the green dragon should always be positioned to the left (East), and the white tiger to the right (West) of any site. The very best site is where the two *ch'i* currents cross or copulate.

The perfect feng-shui location

A perfect site forms a complete horseshoe shape, that is to say where two hill ridges starting from one point run out to the right and left in a graceful curve, their extremities gently turning inwards towards each other (see page 12). Such a formation of hills or mountains is the sure sign of 'the presence of a true dragon'. Obviously we can't all live in idyllic countryside settings, but we can use this ideal to model changes in our present home.

An illustration of this ideal is the favourable situation of the city of Canton (see opposite), which is set in the angle formed by two chains of hills running in gentle curves towards each other, forming a complete horseshoe.

In the classic case of the Ming tombs to the Northwest of Peking the actual names of the hills and ranges betray their feng-shui function, so that the hills to the East of the entrance to the valley of the tombs are called 'Green Dragon Hill', while those to the West of the entrance are called 'White Tiger Hill'. The last resting place of the ancestors of the Chinese Emperor, therefore, is perfectly located.

If these dragon-tiger symbols cannot be perfectly found in the site then the generalized conjunction of 'male' and 'female' ground will do almost as well. Boldly rising elevations are Yang (male), whilst uneven, softly undulating ground is called Yin (female) ground. In areas where such characteristics are not obvious, other features such as tall buildings can take the place of the dragon mountain range, while structures at a lower height symbolize the tiger.

As a consequence of the above set of rules it is apparent that flat land is not propitious from a feng-shui point

The traditionally-shaped plan of Canton faces South on to the river, and is embraced by artificially extended canals and surrounded by supportive hills to the North. Several protective pagodas were built inside the Northern wall.

THE FIVE MOUNTAIN TYPES

The five Elements (and Planets) and the shape of their associated mountain forms:

Fire (Mars): sharp or conical

Wood (Jupiter): round top and high

Earth (Saturn): squarish

Metal (Venus): rounded or oblong

Water (Mercury): crooked or wavy

of view. In fact where flat land surrounds a house, then walls, artificial mounds of earth or lines of trees are often incorporated to the North to improve *ch'i* accumulation qualities.

Mountains

These are the traditional abodes of the immortals, of dragons and gods. Mountains are the pristine source of Yang *ch'i* flows, the most virile and powerful landscape feature and therefore a fit lair for dragons. Rocky outcrops are sometimes seen as dragon bones. It is therefore one of the first requirements of a feng-shui practitioner that he should be able to tell at a moment's glance which star, planet and Element is represented by any given mountain.

Eitel explains that "If a peak rises up bold and straight, running out into a sharp point, it is identified with Mars and declared to represent the Element Fire. If the point of a similarly-shaped mountain is broken off and flat but comparatively narrow, it is said to be the embodiment of Jupiter and to represent the Element Wood. If the top of a mountain forms an extensive plateau, it is the representative of Saturn, and the Element Earth dwells there. If a mountain runs up high but its peak is softly rounded it is called Venus and represents the Element Metal. A mountain whose top has the shape of a cupola is looked upon as the representative of Mercury, and the Element Water rules there."

The **4** Directions, **4** Celestial Animals & **4** Seasons

The most basic Directions are the four compass points North, South, East and West. To simplify remembering the qualities of each Direction, feng-shui practice attributes a symbolic animal to each point.

The green dragon and white tiger locked in an embrace. The best location for a house is the point where they symbolically join or copulate.

Considering the seasons from the Northern Hemisphere, it is obvious that the greatest heat and therefore high summer comes from the South, the direction of the sun at midday. Therefore the Element Fire and the season of Summer are attributed to the South along with the similarly coloured red raven or crimson phoenix, the mythical bird which rises from the ashes of the fire, like the sun rises each day from night. The beneficial feng-shui feature to look for to the South is a low 'footstool' hill or in an urban environment, a low wall.

North

The cold dark North, in contrast, is attributed to Water, whose symbolic animals include the black tortoise or the warrior and whose season is Winter. In the landforms surrounding a site this Direction is most auspicious if occupied by a background of encircling hills, trees, or in an urban environment, a level of higher buildings. These provide solid support to the site and in China would physically protect it from the cold winds of the Northern plains.

East and West

To the East, where the sun rises, is Spring with the azure or green dragon as its symbolic creature. Opposite in the West is Autumn symbolized by the white tiger. The complimentary pairing of the green dragon and the white tiger are considered by feng-shui practitioners to be very important. The dragon is considered to symbolize Yang and will be on the left side of the house or site looking South, whilst the tiger represents Yin and will be found on the right-hand side.

For the feng-shui to be good, buildings or mountains flanking a site to the West and East must have some hint of the characteristics of these two animals. The perfect location, the point where most *ch'i* is accumulated, is supposed to be where the dragon and tiger meet or near the green dragon's genitals.

Centre of the compass

Finally, the fifth Element, Earth is sited at the centre of the compass, acting as a point of balance for the other four. The wind which circulates between them is not considered to be an Element, even though the Ancient Greeks counted Air as one of the Elements.

The Trigrams

Additionally, the full Yang (male)

Trigram of *Ch'ien* represents Summer and the completely Yin (female) Trigram of *K'un* represents Winter.

The Four Seasons

The sun rises in the East, just as the year begins in Spring; reaches its peak in the South (Mid-summer); sets in the West (Autumn); and is dark in the North (Mid-winter).

Spring – East
Summer – South (maximum Yang)
Autumn – West
Winter – North (maximum Yin)

NORTH & SOUTH

Remember that in all traditional feng-shui illustrations (in line with Chinese practice) South is always shown at the top of the page and North at the bottom of the page. However North still means the direction north, even in the Southern Hemisphere. Feng-shui practitioners in Australia, for example, should not reverse these directions simply because of the different Hemisphere.

FOUR CELESTIAL ANIMALS

A stylized view of the four celestial animals in relationship to the compass Directions. The front of the house faces the Red Phoenix in the South and is backed by the Black Tortoise of the North.

SOUTH
Red Bird/Phoenix

EAST
Green Dragon

WEST
White Tiger

N

NORTH
Dark Warrior/Tortoise

The ideal site, or Hsueh, is at the rear of the lowland facing the river and small knoll in the foreground. The high mountain backs the site and the green dragon and white tiger flank it. Note that the green dragon hills are slightly higher than the white tiger range of hills.

The **White Tiger** & the **Green Dragon** in the Landscape

Form School practitioners of feng-shui do more than just locate the compass points North, South, East and West. They try to locate the four celestial animals of each compass point in the landscape.

By locating surrounding landscape features or buildings that fit the symbolic requirements of a good site, and by visualising the four celestial animals embodied in the physical representations, the feng-shui practitioner helps to connect the site with the beneficial influences of the four celestial animals, which offer the occupants of the site their protection.

The landscape betrays the presence of *ch'i* in its positive (Yang) form as a dragon, and in its negative (Yin) form as a tiger. The two different *ch'i* currents in the earth's crust, the one male (positive), the other female (negative), are called, respectively, the green dragon and the white tiger. Facing South, the green dragon must always be to the left (East), and the white tiger to the right (West) of any site. The site is most beneficially placed when the surrounding hills form a horseshoe, that is to say where two ridges of hills starting from one point run out to the right and left in a graceful curve, their extremities gently turning inwards towards each other, one slightly longer than the other. Such a formation of hills or mountains is said to be the sure indicator of a true dragon. Of course in urban areas these hills are replaced by high or low adjoining buildings, each representing the four celestial animals.

Just like the tides of the sea, it is as necessary to receive the influx of life on the incoming tide as it is to lose the waste on the outgoing tide. This is why the dragon and tiger must be balanced, with the incoming tide of the dragon in the ascendant so that the positive virtues of *ch'i* gradually accumulate rather than being washed away (which would be the case if the Yin tiger predominated).

In most cases, the landscape does not form a perfect horseshoe or 'armchair'-shaped surround for the site, but then very few sites are perfect. Feng-shui practitioners who are called in to diagnose the site of a grave will often suggest building a backing made from bricks or concrete behind the grave to protect it from the malign influences of the North. Chinese armchair graves, such as the one above, are very ornate.

The landscape and the city

The feng-shui practitioner looks very precisely at the landscape surrounding a site for a hint of the symbolic presence of the celestial animal forms. For example in a good site it should be possible to look to the East and see a range of mountains or hills representing a recumbent dragon. Then upon looking to the West, the practitioner hopes to see a lower range of hills symbolizing the white tiger. He/she then looks to the North of the site to find a range of hills that act as a 'backing' to the site, symbolizing the tortoise. Finally he will be delighted at what he finds if there is a very low 'footstool' shaped mound to the South symbolizing the phoenix.

In a built-up city, the dragon and the tiger forms are much harder to see. It may simply be that another house to the East will represent the dragon, whilst a lower one to the West will embody the tiger. A low wall to the front, signifying the red phoenix, is often easier to find.

Buildings in a city have to make use of other buildings to represent the support of the tortoise mountain. The World Trade Centre in New York provides this backing for the rest of Manhattan. Note, however, that the communications mast will also generate 'secret arrows'.

CHAPTER 3
THE DIRECTION FINDING ART

Yin & Yang

Yin and Yang are at the root of the Chinese view of the universe. At a simple level they are the female and male principles respectively, husband and wife, man and woman, light and dark, sweet and sour. At a more universal level they are negative and positive.

Unlike the dualism of Christianity, where light is supposed to triumph over darkness, the Chinese are more realistic and pragmatic and know that life is made up of a mixture of light and dark, warmness and coolness. Their ideal is the proper mixture, in the right proportions. The Yin-Yang symbol (see opposite) is the perfect example. At the centre of the cosmological system is unity or *wu-chi* symbolized by a circle. This develops into *t'ai-chi* which is sometimes shown as three alternating rings of dark and light, or in more modern times the Yin-Yang symbol. The middle of the light half (Yang) contains a seed of dark (Yin), and the dark half (Yin) contains a seed of light (Yang). The trick is to obtain a life-giving and sustaining balance.

Applied to the landscape, the hills represent Yang whilst the valleys symbolize Yin. It is therefore not good feng-shui to have a landscape made up of valleys without hills or vice versa. Yang also applies to the sunny side of mountains, whilst Yin symbolizes the darker North-facing slopes.

Yin and Yang are represented in the Chinese classic the *I Ching* as the whole line (Yang) and broken line (Yin). As the whole line is in one part and the broken line is made up of

two parts, Yang is equated to the number one and Yin to the number two: it therefore follows that all odd number are Yang and all even numbers are Yin. Odd numbers are associated with creation (Yang) and even numbers with nourishing and completion (Yin). From a feng-shui point of view Yin implies the fertile shady North side of a hill, whilst Yang is the warm impregnating Southern side. Exactly where these principles fit into feng-shui will become apparent in a later chapter.

Yin governs the Earth and all that is negative, female, dark, water, soft, cold, deadly or still; whilst Yang derives from Heaven and all that is positive, male, light, fiery, hard, warm, living and moving. The combination and permutation of the Yang and the Yin forms the rest of the universe whose life and breath is *ch'i*.

The two breaths of nature, or types of *ch'i*, are essentially one breath. They make up the male and female principles: when they unite they constitute the beginning or birth of things; when they disperse they cause decay, dissolution and death.

The Trigrams

From the Yin and the Yang come the eight Trigrams (see pages 30-31), each of which are made up of three lines on top of each other, each line being either whole (Yang) or broken (Yin). Of these Trigrams the male all-Yang Trigram, made of three whole lines, is called *Ch'ien* or Heaven, while the *K'un* all-Yin Trigram is made up of three broken lines and represents Earth. The other six Trigrams are made up of a mixture of both Yin and Yang.

The Elements

Yin and Yang interact with each other to produce the next level of complexity, the five Elements: Water, Fire, Wood, Metal and Earth (see pages 32-33). Finally from these Elements come what the Taoists call 'the ten thousand myriad things' or the rest of creation.

Ch'ien:

The Heaven Trigram Ch'ien *is made up of three Yang (unbroken) lines. This Trigram is completely Yang.*

K'un:

The Earth Trigram K'un *is made up of three Yin (broken) lines. This Trigram is completely Yin.*

*Yin and Yang join to generate the five Elements
Water, Fire, Wood, Metal and Earth.*

The **8** Ancient Trigrams

The positive and negative qualities of Yin and Yang are expressed as either a solid line (Yang) or a broken line (Yin). These lines taken three at a time provide eight possible combinations of Yin and Yang which are known as the eight Trigrams.

It is said that the sage Fu Hsi invented the Trigrams more than 4000 years ago. Later King Wen (circa 1150 BC) combined each of the eight Trigrams with each of the others to produce 64 hexagrams. Each of these hexagrams had a textual interpretation added to them, first by the Duke of Chou and later by Confucius, forming the Chinese classic the *I Ching* (also known as the *Classic of Changes*).

Each of the eight ancient Trigrams has a specific meaning (see box, opposite). Ranging from *Ch'ien*, which consists of three unbroken lines and symbolizes Yang, the father or head of the household, through to three broken lines, *K'un,* which symbolizes Yin and Mother Earth.

The Trigrams are combined one with another to form eight by eight combinations, also known as the 64 hexagrams of the *I Ching*. This book is central to the Chinese view of the universe and is also used as an instrument of divination. It is said that all changes can be predicted from these 64 hexagrams.

Sites and houses

When considering the site of a property or home the Trigrams are laid out in the Later Heaven Sequence (see pages 34-35), with the Trigram *Li* facing South. The Trigrams are used to evaluate watercourse entry and exit points. In other words, the feng-shui compass is used to determine the sector in which a stream or pond first becomes visible, and the sector from which it finally drains away out of sight. The Trigrams also illustrate the qualities which may be associated with each source of water *ch'i* and how it will affect the site.

A traditional view of the sage Fu Hsi as a mountain, an indication of the intimate relationship between the Trigrams he invented and the feng-shui landscape.

THE TRIGRAMS

Ch'ien corresponds to immobility and strength. It represents a horse; the head; the heavenly sphere; the father; a prince; roundness; jade; metal; the fruit of trees; and red colours.

Chen indicates motion; a dragon, i.e. the animal of the East in the Later Heaven Sequence (see pages 34-35); the feet; the eldest son; thunder; development; high roads; decision; vehemence; bamboo; rushes; and dark-yellow colours.

Tui means pleasure; a sheep; the mouth; the youngest daughter; spiritual mediums; the tongue; and a concubine.

K'an signifies peril; a pig; the ears; the middle son; channels and streams; hidden things; a bow; a wheel; anxiety; pain in the ears; high spirits; a drooping head; thieves; strong trees; and the colour blood-red.

K'un represents docility; bovine cattle; the belly; the mother; Mother Earth; cloth; cauldrons; parsimony; large carts; figures; a multitude; a handle; and the colour black.

Sun means penetration; a fowl; the thighs; the eldest daughter; wood; wind; length; height; a backwards and forwards motion; bald-headedness; a broad forehead; and the colour white.

Ken indicates stoppage; a dog; the hands; the youngest son; paths and roads; small rocks; gates; fruits and cucumbers; porters or eunuchs; finger rings; rats; and birds with large bills.

Li means beauty; brightness; a pheasant, the bird of the South in the Later Heaven Sequence; eyes; the middle daughter; the sun; lightning; helmets; spears and swords; dryness; crabs; spiral uni-valves; and mussels.

Inside the home

The Trigrams provide indications of the best rooms for specific purposes or for specific members of the family. As each Trigram is associated with one or other family member so he/she is better placed if his/her bedroom is located in the corresponding sector of the house, or one which does not conflict with his/her Trigram.

For feng-shui the significance of, for example, the relationship between the Trigrams and family members is of vital importance when considering which member of a family will receive the most benefit by having his or her representative Trigram aligned with the main door of the house (see pages 56-57).

THE PA KUA

The Pa Kua is an octagonal-shaped symbol which contains the four cardinal Directions and the four intercardinal Directions of the compass, plus the Elements and the Trigrams. Fire is opposite to Water. The two Trigrams attributed to Earth are opposite each other, with K'un being the stronger Yin Earth Trigram. Both pairs of Wood and Metal Trigrams are adjacent to each other. Ch'ien being all Yang is obviously the stronger of the two Metal Trigrams.

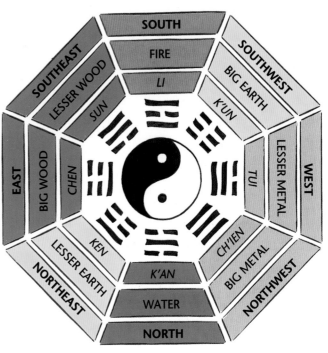

Using the 5 Elements

The 5 Elements, Fire, Water, Wood, Metal and Earth, evolve out of Yin and Yang. By Elements the Chinese meant the principle energies behind the manifest physical universe. The Element Wood therefore is not the same as a chunk of timber, but is the animating principle that dwells in any forest or vegetation, or as Dylan Thomas put it "the force that through the green fuse drives the flower".

THE 5 ELEMENTS

The qualities of the five Elements:

The Chinese term for the Elements is *hsing,* which indicates movement, so perhaps 'the five moving agents' might be a more appropriate name for them. This term reinforces the concept that the Elements generate and destroy each other in a continuous cycle. Like the Trigrams and hexagrams of the *I Ching,* these are symbols of change and transformation, and can be used to improve the feng-shui of your home.

All the Elements are related to and interact with each other. Wood represents the essence of all vegetation, which is fed by Water, which covers and binds the Earth, which is cut down by Metal implements, which ignite to give Fire. Water is understood to be all forms of fluid including the liquefaction of Metal within the Earth. Earth is understood to mean all mixed, impure and inanimate substances including the ash produced by Fire.

The relationship between the five Elements and the Directions of the compass is important for the practice of feng-shui, and the knowledge of how each Element relates to the others helps to solve practical feng-shui problems. The colours of the Elements relate to interior decoration and suggest how certain Elements and their effects can be stimulated by using colour (see pages 64-65).

The Chinese thought that the Elements combined in differing quantities to form everything found in nature, and hence the Elements were the animating principles behind the material manifestation of nature.

The Elements and you

On a personal level each of us has an Element associated with our year of birth (see pages 50-51). If you are born in an Earth year then it will be very sensible to surround your home with things which are symbolic of Earth, or even better the Element which generates Earth (see The Production Cycle, page 37). As Fire creates Earth it would be a good Element to emphasize. Wood on the other hand destroys Earth (see The Destruction Cycle, page 37) and would not be a

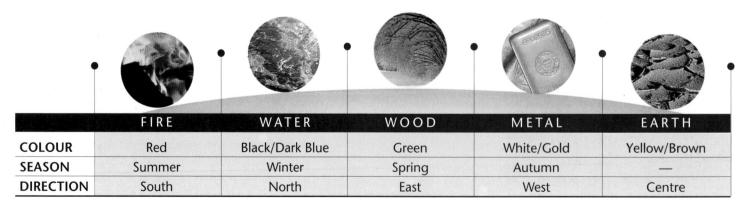

	FIRE	WATER	WOOD	METAL	EARTH
COLOUR	Red	Black/Dark Blue	Green	White/Gold	Yellow/Brown
SEASON	Summer	Winter	Spring	Autumn	—
DIRECTION	South	North	East	West	Centre

good Element to emphasize in your home. If you are a Fire person, then a Water-oriented environment might not be the best as Water destroys Fire.

In addition, everyone has an Element associated with their month, day and hour of birth. Taken with the year, this gives the eight character Elemental make up of the individual, the basis of a Chinese horoscope. But the Element of the year of birth is the most important in a feng-shui context.

CASE STUDY

Sue was a primary school teacher born in 1961. She was instinctively drawn to interiors which emphasized metal and she particularly liked dark colours. However, she felt distinctly uncomfortable in rooms decorated in strong red colours. It was not until she worked out her Chinese birth dates that she understood why she felt this way. From the instructions given on pages 50-51 she calculated that the Element of the year of her birth was Metal. Metal is created by Water, which has an affinity for dark colours (see the chart on the opposite page). On the other hand Metal is destroyed by Fire which is associated with strong red spectrum colours.

TABLE OF ELEMENTS, TRIGRAMS, ANIMALS, EMBLEMS & SEASONS

TRIGRAM		ELEMENT	ASSOCIATED ANIMAL	EMBLEM	ASSOCIATED SEASON	INTERPRETATION
	Ch'ien	Metal	Dragon, Horse	Heaven	Late Autumn	Creative; strength; roundness; vitality
	K'un	Earth	Mare, Ox	Earth	Late Summer-Early Autumn	Receptive; yielding; nourishment
	Chen	Wood	Galloping Horse, Flying Dragon	Thunder	Spring	Movement; arousal
	K'an	Water	Pig	Moon & Water	Mid-winter	Curved objects; flowing water; danger
	Ken	Lesser Earth	Dog, Rat, Black-billed Birds	Mountain	Early Spring	Steadiness; stillness; gates; fruits; seeds
	Sun	Lesser Wood	Hen	Wind	Early Summer	Gentleness; penetration; growth; vegetative growth
	Li	Fire	Pheasant, Toad, Crab, Snail, Tortoise	Sun & Lightning	Summer	Adherence; dependence; weapons; drought; brightness
	Tui	Lesser Metal	Sheep	Lake & Seawater	Mid-autumn	Joy; serenity; reflections & mirror images

The 8 Pa Kua Directions

The Pa Kua (or Ba Gua if you prefer the modern transliteration of the Chinese) is the basic tool of Compass School feng-shui. It is an eight-sided figure, which allocates each of the eight Trigrams to the eight compass Directions, to the four cardinal points of the compass and to the four intercardinal points.

One Chinese convention we will adhere to in this book is illustrating floor plans of houses together with the Pa Kua symbol showing the South to the top of the page and the North to the bottom, rather than the other way around as in the Western world. However, North still means the direction North, even in the Southern Hemisphere. The disadvantage of this is that this is the reverse of the convention used in all modern occidental maps. Maps were not always shown with North at the top: it is a fairly modern convention. The advantage of showing South at the top is that this is the direction you would look out of your front door if you were in a house with an ideal South-facing location.

The Later Heaven Sequence

The Pa Kua in the Later Heaven Sequence (see box, opposite) shows which Trigram (see page 31) is allocated to which compass point. These Pa Kua directions are very versatile. They can be applied either to a whole city, to a whole house or its garden, or a flat in the house or just to a room in a flat. It is effective at each of these levels because it determines Directions and a Direction is the same whether viewed from a single room in the smallest flat or from the walls of a whole city.

The Pa Kua and your home

By placing the Pa Kua symbol over a plan of your home you can divide it up into eight sectors, North, South, East, West, Southwest, Southeast, Northwest and Northeast. The eight sectors of the Pa Kua correspond to an area in your life (see The Pa Kua Sectors, opposite).

Now we begin to connect the apparently abstract Chinese symbols with your home and aspirations. By orientating the top of the Pa Kua to

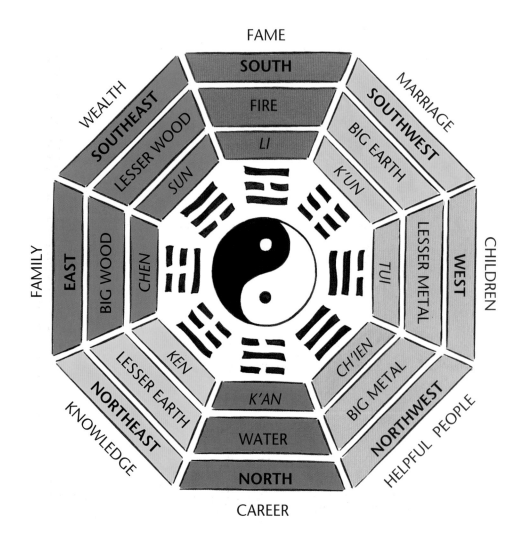

The key to the Pa Kua: the correlation between the compass Directions, Trigrams, life aspirations, Elements and colours.

THE TWO ARRANGEMENTS OF THE PA KUA

There are two traditional orders in which the Trigrams are paired up with the compass points. These two arrangements are called the Earlier Heaven Sequence and the Later Heaven Sequence.

The difference between these is that the Earlier Heaven Sequence is the ancient or ideal heavenly order and is used mainly in the feng-shui of tombs or grave sites. It has *Ch'ien* or the Heaven/Father Trigram located in the South opposite to *K'un* or the Earth/Mother Trigram located in the North. These Trigrams are exact opposites of each other, as are the Fire (East) and Water (West) Trigrams of the other axis. This arrangement is highly symmetrical, and the Northwest/Southeast and Southwest/Northeast Trigram pairs are also exact opposites.

Unfortunately the arrangement of Trigrams for the dwelling places of the living is less perfect, and is represented by the Later Heaven Sequence devised by King Wen. The Later Heaven Sequence however is important for the feng-shui of houses and gardens, and is therefore of most interest to us. Most feng-shui books give both sequences, which is very confusing. We will only use the Later Heaven Sequence in this book as this is the one needed for determining home and town feng-shui.

Earlier Heaven Sequence

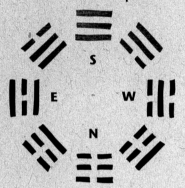

Later Heaven Sequence

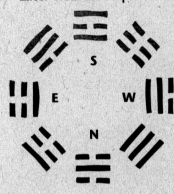

THE PA KUA SECTORS

THE 8 SECTORS OF THE PA KUA EACH CORRESPOND TO A LIFE ASPIRATION

South	fame
Southwest	marital happiness & relationships
West	children
Northwest	new beginnings & mentors
North	career prospects
Northeast	education
East	family relationships & health
Southeast	wealth & prosperity

the South compass Direction of the plan of your home, office or room you get eight even sectors, each attributed to a different facet of your life. In an L-shaped house or flat, then one or more of the Pa Kua sectors will be missing.

The Pa Kua on this home plan shows the Trigram K'un in the Southwest study, Chen in the East-facing kitchen and K'an at the North-facing front door.

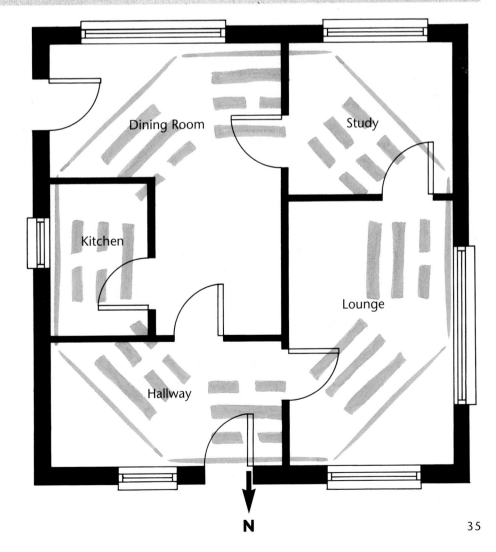

Production & Destruction of the 5 Elements

The five Elements are connected together in two cycles. The first, the Production Cycle, explains which Element generates the next and the second, the Destruction Cycle, demonstrates which Element destroys another. These cycles are one of the most important keys to the practice of feng-shui as they offer practical guidance on how to improve your personal feng-shui.

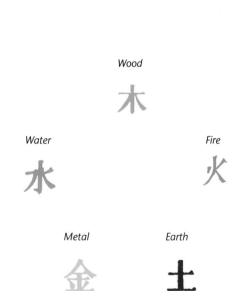

Wood

木

Water

水

Fire

火

Metal

金

Earth

土

The Chinese characters for the five Elements in the order of the Production Cycle. Note the close similarity of the symbols for the 'natural' Elements Water, Wood and Fire.

The Production Cycle works like this: Wood burns to produce Fire, which results in ash (or Earth) in which Metal may be found. Metal is also found in the veins of the earth from which (according to Chinese thought) sprang the underground streams (Water) which nourish vegetation and produce Wood.

Each Element destroys another in the Destruction Cycle shown, so that in feng-shui theory the destroyer is hostile to the destroyed Element.

These cycles are important not just as theory, but because they provide the key to enhancing or modifying the feng-shui of your home. The rule is that to enhance a sector you add to its corresponding Element, and to stimulate this Element you add the Element that produces it. For example, assuming that you wanted to stimulate your wealth sector. From the Pa Kua (see pages 34-35) it is apparent that the sector of your home associated with wealth is the Southeast and that this sector is associated with the Element of Wood (see the diagram on page 34).

Looking at the Production Cycle you can see that the Element that produces Wood is Water. Therefore the addition of a Water feature, such as a fish tank or a small fountain, in the Southeast sector will strengthen Wood in that quarter and thus stimulate wealth luck and prosperity. That is how the Production Cycle can work to your advantage. If on the other hand you installed a Metal feature in the Southeast sector, then you would destroy the Element of Wood in this sector (see the Destruction Cycle, opposite), reducing your chances of increasing your wealth.

The Destruction Cycle
This cycle is a little more tricky to use. Metal cuts down and destroys Wood. Wood draws its essence from and destroys Earth. Earth in turn is destroyed by Water. Water in turn

CASE STUDY

Annette found that she was having difficulty establishing a long term relationship – boyfriends came and went. She discovered that according to feng-shui principles the Southwest quarter was the quarter which related to relationships and marriage, and the associated Element was Earth. She checked up on the Production Cycle of the Elements and found that Fire creates Earth.

She reasoned that to increase the potential of a long term relationship or marriage she needed to add Fire to her Southwest quarter to produce more of the Earth Element. Accordingly, she introduced more red into the decor of the Southwest corner of her living room. She also lit candles in this quarter, thus introducing Fire, and moved a red-shaded lamp to this corner. Within two weeks she found herself in a steady relationship which looks like becoming permanent.

extinguishes and destroys Fire. Fire melts and destroys Metal, which brings us back to the beginning of the Destructive Cycle.

Using this cycle you could minimize the effects of a particular Element by symbolically adding the Element that destroys it. For example an overabundance of Fire in one sector of the house could be reduced by adding a Water feature, as Water destroys Fire. There is a more subtle way of achieving this end by using the Element that is produced by the Element you are seeking to reduce. Thus applying Earth to a sector will reduce an overabundance of the Element Fire (see Production Cycle above).

THE CYCLES OF THE ELEMENTS

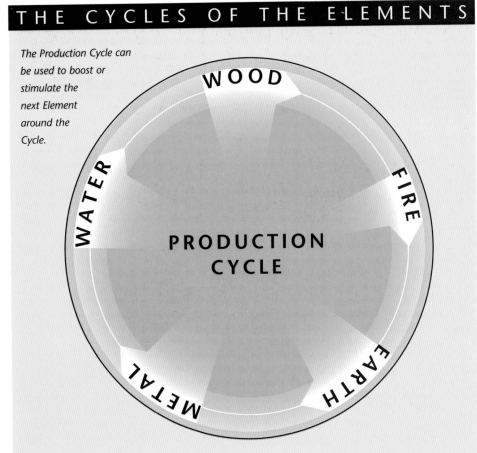

The Production Cycle can be used to boost or stimulate the next Element around the Cycle.

PRODUCTION CYCLE

WOOD · FIRE · EARTH · METAL · WATER

The Destruction Cycle can be used to reduce or modify Elements by using the destroying Element in the cycle.

DESTRUCTION CYCLE

WOOD · EARTH · WATER · FIRE · METAL

The Lo Shu Magic Square

The Lo Shu is one of the most ancient tools of feng-shui. The Lo Shu is a magic square with a 3 x 3 grid of nine chambers which helps the feng-shui practitioner to analyse a house or flat, and predict flux and changes for its occupants.

The turtle is a very mystical Chinese animal, often found in hundreds in pools near Buddhist temples. The turtle is reputed to have brought the Lo Shu formula to man around 2205 BC.

The Lo Shu square is a 'magic' square because the numbers placed in its nine chambers add up to 15 regardless of which direction you add them up, even diagonally. The numbers in the Lo Shu are used in a number of feng-shui formulae, some of which will be explained in later chapters.

Tradition says that the image of the Lo Shu square was first seen by the sage Yu who saw it inscribed on the shell of a turtle arising from the Lo river about 2205 BC.

What does it do?

The Lo Shu neatly coincides with the eight Trigrams arranged in the Later Heaven Sequence of the Pa Kua (see pages 34-35), plus a central chamber which is assigned to Earth. The chamber which contains the number 9 is aligned with the South and number 1 with the North.

The Lo Shu is used extensively in Compass School feng-shui. It is used like the Pa Kua to divide up the house into nine sectors, or it can be used on a smaller scale to divide a room into nine sectors.

The Eras of the *Lo Shu*

One of the secrets of the Lo Shu is that it unlocks the time dimension for feng-shui, and allows practitioners to decide precisely when is the best time to make changes to the site, the home or the interior decoration.

In drawing up a feng-shui analysis of a house, the original Lo Shu may be used, but the order of the numbers is modified over time. Time is divided into Eras of 60 years, consisting of three cycles of 20 years. During each cycle the order of numbers differs from the original Lo Shu. The current cycle is the seventh which began in 1984 and will end in 2003. For the duration of this cycle, every house built during this time will have a 7 at the centre of its Lo Shu, with the other numbers moved around in a specific order (see The Current Lo Shu, opposite). However the basic pattern is all we need to know.

The numbers change in the Lo Shu in a logical manner from Era to Era. If you connect up the nine chambers in numeric order, you get a diagram which shows the order in which the numbers move from Era to Era (see The Pattern of Numbers, opposite).

Compass School: *Wang Chih*

Not until the rise of the Sung dynasty were all the elements of feng-shui gathered into one methodical system which combined every form of influence that heaven and earth were supposed to have on human affairs. The Directions and Positions School or Compass School is also referred to as the Fukien School of feng-shui. This School places great stress on the Pa Kua, the eight Trigrams, the Heavenly Stems and Earthly Branches and the Constellations (more of which later), assigning a place of minor importance to the landscape configurations of the earth. Wang Chih (circa AD 960) was an early master of the Compass School.

THE LO SHU SQUARE AROUND THE WORLD

As well as in China, the Lo Shu square has been part of the magical traditions of the Middle East and Europe for at least 2000 years. In Western magic derived from ancient Hebrew traditions, a square with exactly the same numbers is known as the square of the planet Saturn and under some circumstances also as the square of the Earth. In the West there are seven planetary squares and they were used to generate the signs which were used to control the spirits of the planets. The zig-zag arrow pattern is the seal of Saturn or Earth.

Another interesting cross-cultural coincidence is that Shu is the Egyptian god of the atmosphere, who along with Tefnut rules the winds and the movement of moisture through the atmosphere. Control of the clouds and the moisture in the air is very much a concern of feng-shui and the Lo Shu square.

THE ORIGINAL LO SHU

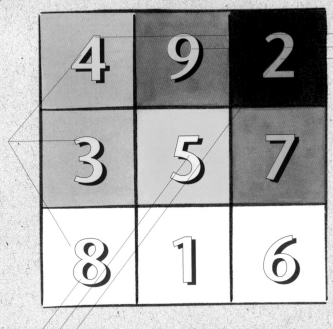

Adding the numbers together vertically equals 15

Adding the numbers horizontally equals 15

Adding the numbers diagonally equals 15

The archetypal Lo Shu arrangement of the numbers 1 to 9. There are eight different ways of adding them together, each time producing 15. The 24 Directions (see pages 42-43) multiplied by 15 give the 360° measurement of the circle.

THE CURRENT LO SHU

SOUTH

6	2	4
5	7	9
1	3	8

In each period the numbers 'fly' around the Lo Shu. During the Cycle from 1984 to 2003 the numbers reside in the Lo Shu squares as above. The number 7 falls in the centre and is therefore called the reigning number.

THE PATTERN OF NUMBERS

The arrows follow the numbers from 1 to 9 tracing out the ancient square of Saturn or Earth. The numbers move or 'fly' around the Lo Shu following the order indicated by the arrows.

The 10 Heavenly Stems & 12 Earthly Branches

The 10 Heavenly Stems and 12 Earthly Branches are key categories in feng-shui, the Chinese calendar and cosmology. The Stems and Branches are used to measure time and direction.

THE 10 HEAVENLY STEMS		
NUMBER	NAME	ELEMENT
1	甲 chia	Wood
2	乙 i	
3	丙 ping	Fire
4	丁 ting	
5	午 wu	Earth
6	己 chi	
7	庚 keng	Metal
8	辛 hsin	
9	壬 jen	Water
10	癸 kuei	

The ten Heavenly Stems are sometimes referred to as 'containing water'. Remember that even in the West the phrase 'Milky Way' applies to the stars, showing an unacknowledged connection between the stars and milk or water. The Egyptians also saw the stars as the milk from the breasts of Nuit, the goddess of the sky.

Four of the Heavenly Stems are considered lucky, and four unlucky:

Unlucky stems	Lucky Stems
1	3
2	4
9	7
10	8

The relative luck of the Stems is related to their association with the Trigrams (see page 31). The unlucky Stems 1, 2, 9 and 10 are associated with the *Ch'ien* and *K'un* Trigrams which are unlucky because they are overwhelmingly Yang and Yin respectively with no mixture or balance. On the other hand, because Stems 3, 4, 7 and 8 are associated with the *Ken* and *Sun* Trigrams which have a suitable mixture of Yin and Yang, they are considered to be lucky.

Stems 1 and 9 are seen as Yang 'orphans', that is, children left alone in the world who therefore need to extend their own self-reliance in a very Yang way.

Stems 2 and 10 symbolize Yin emptiness: quite the reverse of stems 1 and 9, but again an undesirable state, with no balance asserting itself in the context of their symbology. Orphan-emptiness literally means 'unlucky' in Chinese.

Stems 3 and 7 represent Yang prosperity – again a lucky blend. 'Prosperity-assistance' is the Chinese compound word for 'lucky'.

Stems 5 and 6 represent the centre and do not partake of any particular Direction. On the scale of numbers 1 to 10 they also stand at the middle and are allocated to no Trigram in particular as of course there are only eight Trigrams to go around ten Stems. The Stems also stand for the numerals from 1 to 10 or if grouped in Yin-Yang pairs they stand for the five Elements, each being either a 'big' or 'lesser' version of each Element.

The 12 Earthly Branches

The twelve Earthly Branches give specific information about time and place. The twelve main points on the compass are those allocated to the twelve Earthly Branches and their basic function is to mark the Directions. Taken on their own the Branches also indicate the twelve two-hour divisions of the day as well as the twelve months of the year.

A year, a month and an hour can all be designated by one of the twelve Earthly Branches, which can then in turn signify a Direction of the compass for each of these times.

The seasons fit in naturally with the Branches and indicate the best times of the year for initiating projects connected with building or buying. The water solstice occurs halfway through Branch *tzu* (due North) which is the beginning of the Chinese New Year, and the rest of the Branches follow in order allocating the parts of the compass to the time of the year through *mao* due East (Spring), *wu* due South (Midsummer) and *yu* due West (Autumn).

When the twelve Earthly Branches interact with five of the ten Heavenly Stems they become the 60 Sexagenary figures (see pages 48-49) which are used both on the feng-shui compass and for marking off the years.

THE 12 EARTHLY BRANCHES

The 12 Earthly Branches with their associated Directions, Roman numbers and 'zodiacal' animal. Note that the Branches and Stems are combined on page 42 to form the full 24 Directions of the feng-shui compass.

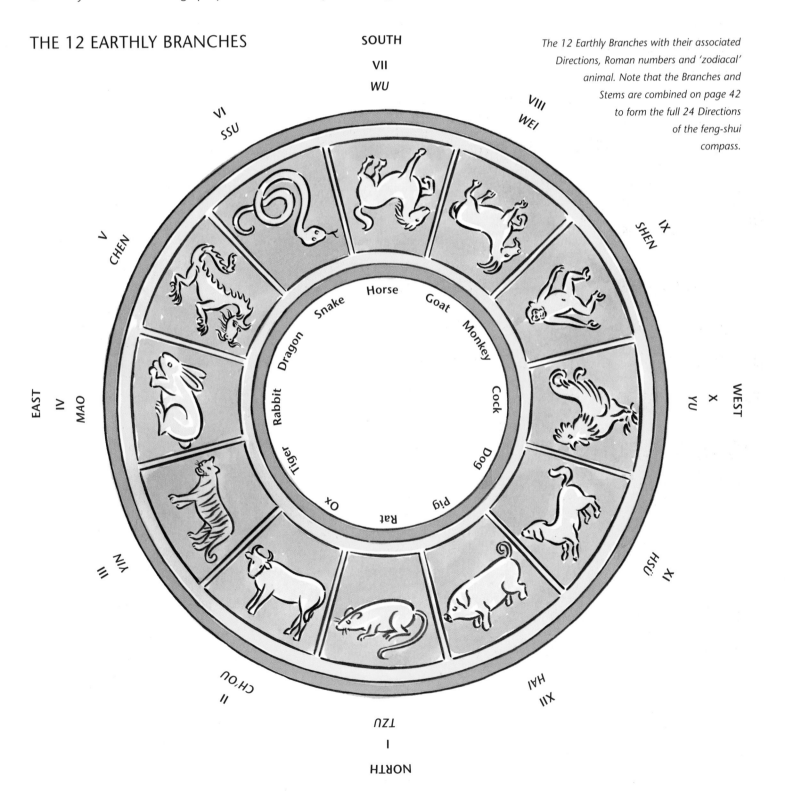

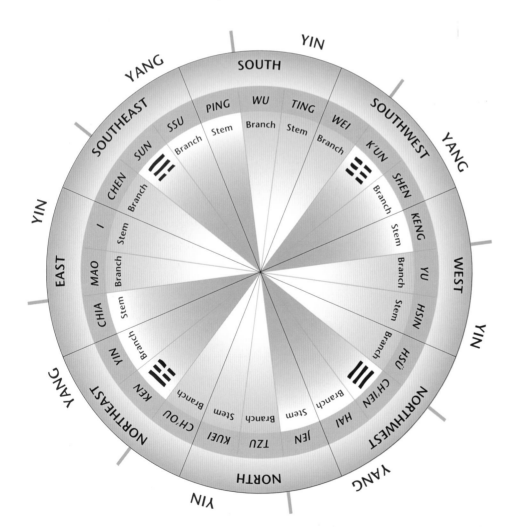

風水
FENG-SHUI

The **24** Compass Directions

The most basic division of the *lo p'an* or feng-shui compass is by the eight Trigrams. Then the eight Trigrams are sub-divided into 24 compass Directions, three Directions for each cardinal point North, South, East and West, and three Directions for each intercardinal point, Southwest, Northwest, Southeast and Northeast.

Each of the 24 compass Directions is classed as either Yin or Yang. Rather confusingly these 24 compass Directions are also made up of three other sets of symbols:

- 12 Earthly Branches
- 8 of the 10 Heavenly Stems
- 4 of the 8 Trigrams

However, this is not as complicated as it sounds as four Trigrams mark the intercardinal points, and four Branches mark the cardinal points. The two missing Heavenly Stems are reserved for the Element of Earth at the centre of the compass.

These 24 Directions are the key to the feng-shui compass. It also contains the 24 Directions that appear on Chinese mariners' compasses (see box, opposite). Most feng-shui compasses feature the ring of 24 Directions three times. It is not necessary to remember the Chinese name of each Direction, but understanding its qualities helps with further feng-shui analysis.

THE BASIC COMPASS DIRECTIONS

This is one of the most important illustrations in the book because it ties together all of the Compass School symbology you have learnt up to this page. On the outside, it first shows the whole circle divided up into Yin and Yang sectors (see pages 28-29). The next ring shows the points of the compass. The four 'corner points', Northwest, Southwest, Southeast and Southwest each have one of the Trigrams (see page 31) attributed to it. The rest of the 24 Compass Directions have either a Branch or Stem (see pages 40-41) attributed to them.

THE 24 DIRECTIONS OF THE COMPASS ARE AS FOLLOWS:

DIRECTION	CHINESE NAME	WHAT IT IS	YIN OR YANG	RANGE OF COMPASS DEGREES	CHINESE CHARACTER
South	*Ping*	Stem	Yang	157.5-172.5	丙
	Wu	**Branch**	**Yin**	**172.5-187.5**	午
	Ting	Stem	Yin	187.5-202.5	丁
Southwest	*Wei*	Branch	Yin	202.5-217.5	未
	K'un	**Trigram**	**Yang**	**217.5-232.5**	坤
	Shen	Branch	Yang	232.5-247.5	申
West	*Keng*	Stem	Yang	247.5-262.5	庚
	Yu	**Branch**	**Yin**	**262.5-277.5**	酉
	Hsin	Stem	Yin	277.5-292.5	辛
Northwest	*Hsu*	Branch	Yin	292.5-307.5	戌
	Ch'ien	**Trigram**	**Yang**	**307.5-322.5**	乾
	Hai	Branch	Yang	322.5-337.5	亥
North	*Jen*	Stem	Yang	337.5-352.5	壬
	Tzu	**Branch**	**Yin**	**352.5-7.5**	子
	Kuei	Stem	Yin	7.5-22.5	癸
Northeast	*Ch'ou*	Branch	Yin	22.5-37.5	丑
	Ken	**Trigram**	**Yang**	**37.5-52.5**	艮
	Yin	Branch	Yang	52.5-67.5	寅
East	*Chia*	Stem	Yang	67.5-82.5	甲
	Mao	**Branch**	**Yin**	**82.5-97.5**	卯
	I	Stem	Yin	97.5-112.5	乙
Southeast	*Chen*	Branch	Yin	112.5-127.5	辰
	Sun	**Trigram**	**Yang**	**127.5-142.5**	巽
	Ssu	Branch	Yang	142.5-157.5	巳

Each of the eight cardinal and intercardinal points is printed in bold in the table above. Each of the four intercardinal points, Southwest, Southeast, Northwest and Northeast, retains its own Trigram from the Later Heaven Sequence (see pages 34-35). These four Trigrams are flanked on either side by one of the Earthly Branches. Each of the cardinal points also take a Branch, flanked on either side by a Heavenly Stem. The reason why these different types of symbols are mixed is not important at this time.

If you look at the fourth column of the table above you can see that three Yang Directions alternate with three Yin Directions. Also if you ignore the four Trigrams, the Earthly Branches alternate with the Heavenly Stems. These 24 compass Directions become important when we come to look at the orientation of the house, and which of these 24 Directions it faces.

For precision readings with a Western compass, the corresponding degrees are listed in the table above. Thus, if a particular mountain top was visible at 146°, we would be able to tell from the above table that the corresponding Yang Branch in the Southeast sector is *Ssu*.

CH'I FLOWS

INTERACTION BETWEEN FORM SCHOOL AND COMPASS SCHOOL

The vital *ch'i* which feeds the life on the surface of the earth flows along the lines of the hill ridges, is blown by the wind, and is carried by the water as well as through the underground veins of the earth. The direction from which this *ch'i* flows gives it different qualities.

To determine the resultant mix of these *ch'i* flows the site is often looked upon as a disc or compass card with flows of *ch'i* entering or leaving from one of the 24 Directions. The Compass School of thought lays particular stress upon the exact degrees of entry and exit of *ch'i* in relation to the centre. Here the Compass School approach is in fact complementary to the Form School approach which tends to rely more on the intuitive assessment made by the feng-shui practitioner.

A simple mariner's compass showing the 24 Chinese characters for the Directions.

A Simple Feng-shui Compass

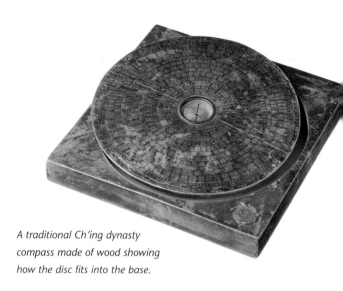

A traditional Ch'ing dynasty compass made of wood showing how the disc fits into the base.

After using Form School or landscape feng-shui to evaluate the surroundings of the site, the next step is to use a feng-shui compass. The compass was not necessarily first used in China as a navigational instrument. It may well have been used to determine the direction of the earth's magnetic field, or even for feng-shui purposes.

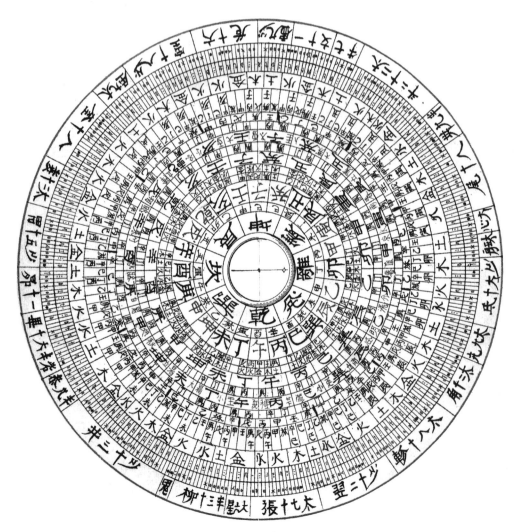

The feng-shui compass is called a *lo p'an* and it is much more complex than a Western maritime compass. *Lo p'ans* are obtainable through specialist feng-shui shops, or religious supply shops in countries like Singapore.

A full feng-shui compass

The compass is in a way an extension of the Pa Kua circle of Trigrams (see pages 34–35). A full feng-shui compass can have as many as 36 rings with between eight and 365 divisions on each ring. They are usually made of wood and fit into a square wooden base. In the centre of the circular disc is a glass-covered depression called the Heaven Pool containing the magnetic needle, painted so that it points to the South (or a small circle at the end of the needle should be lined up with two

A FULL LO P'AN

A 17-ring nineteenth century lo p'an *showing how complex a full feng-shui compass can be.*

small dots on the floor of the Heaven Pool which indicate magnetic North). A North-South line is drawn on the floor of the Heaven Pool. When the needle is exactly aligned with this line, with the red end pointing South, then the compass is correctly aligned.

A simple feng-shui compass

The inner ring of a simple *lo p'an* is divided up into the eight Trigrams (see page 31). The next couple of rings are combinations of the Elements (see pages 32-33), the numbers of the Lo Shu Magic Square (see pages 38-39) and the 24 compass Directions (see pages 42-43). The inner rings of the compass are the only ones of immediate interest, as they relate to Yang feng-shui, or houses and cities. The middle and outer rings are more concerned with Yin feng-shui, the feng-shui of graves.

The *lo p'an* and your home

To assess the feng-shui qualities of your home, or any site, the first step is to identify each of the compass Directions. To do this you need a compass. This does not have to be a feng-shui compass, and can be anything from an ordinary hiking or orienteering compass through to an expensive military compass which gives exact readings in degrees. Alternatively, you can use a simple feng-shui compass made up of 7 rings or an extremely complex 36-ringed antique feng-shui compass, but a simple compass will do.

First use the compass to check for South, remembering that we are talking about the Direction in which a compass points not map South which is approximately 7.5 degrees different.

The square base into which the compass is set has two precisely aligned cross hairs intersecting at right angles. These cross hairs are used to indicate the reading on the rings.

THE INNER 4 RINGS OF A TYPICAL LO P'AN

In contrast to the full 17-ring lo p'an *compass shown on the opposite page, the box to the right shows the 7 rings in a basic* lo p'an. *The most important inner four rings are analysed graphically below. The Earthly Branches are shown as Roman numerals and the Heavenly Stems as ordinary numbers, while the Trigrams appear in the usual form.*

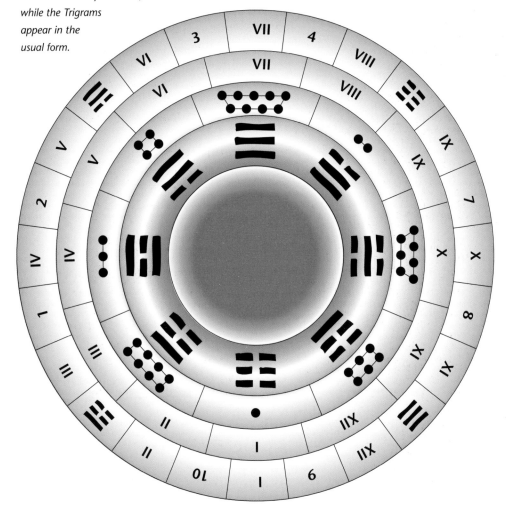

LO P'AN

A BASIC *LO P'AN* SHOULD HAVE THE FOLLOWING 7 RINGS:

0 Heaven Pool – the actual compass needle and well.

1 The 8 Trigrams arranged in the Earlier Heaven Sequence.

2 8 of the 9 numbers of the Lo Shu Magic Square are represented symbolically, so that 1 is represented by one dot, 2 by two dots connected by a line, and so on. As 5 applies to the centre it is not represented in this circle.

3 The 12 Earthly Branches (see pages 40-41).

4 The 24 Directions of the Chinese compass, made up of Branches, Stems and Trigrams.

5 The 24 *Chieh ch'i* or fortnightly divisions of the Solar calendar.

6 The 60 Dragons or Sexagenary characters, namely the 5 Heavenly Stems matched with the 12 Earthly Branches.

7 The 28 unevenly spaced *hsiu* or Chinese constellations.

Using the Feng-shui Compass

A modern feng-shui compass in the author's collection.

The first reading to be taken with the compass is the direction that the front door of the house faces: this is called the Facing Direction. The opposite direction to this is known as the Mountain or Siting Direction and it is 180° from the Facing Direction.

The 24 Directions of the compass are shown on page 42. You can take a reading of the Facing Direction with either:

1 a traditional Chinese *lo p'an* using the ring showing the 24 Directions
2 a homemade *lo p'an* using a simple compass and a cardboard disc with a copy of the illustration on page 45 pasted to it
3 a Western hiking compass which reads off exact degrees, read in conjunction with the table on page 43.

In each case, position yourself just inside your open front door looking outwards. The procedure differs slightly depending upon the equipment used.

A traditional *Lo P'an*

There are several steps to using a traditional *lo p'an*. First the outer square base should be lined up parallel with the front door, so that one of the cross hairs points out of the door at right angles to the threshold.

A feng-shui master judging the exact alignment of a site using a red string fixed between two staves above a compass.

Then the inner circular disc should be rotated until the magnetic needle lines up with the line underneath it. Usually the small circle at one end of the needle should be aligned with the two red dots on the floor of the Heaven Pool. It is important to line the needle up precisely. Then the cross hair pointing out of the front door will indicate the Facing Direction.

A homemade *Lo P'an*

A *lo p'an* can be made from a cardboard ring with the 24 Directions marked upon it with a hiking compass mounted in the middle. First turn the compass until the north-pointing needle indicates North. Then turn the cardboard ring until the centre of Direction *tzu* (see page 42) also lines up with North. Then sight from the centre of the compass in the Facing Direction (the Direction pointing out of the front door is the Facing Direction).

A Western hiking compass

Use a hiking compass with a sight which reads exact

A Western hiking compass which enables you to take a siting on a specific landform feature, and read off the exact number of degrees.

THE COMPASS DIRECTIONS APPLIED TO A HOUSE

Applying the basic four rings of the compass to this house plan, the Facing Direction pointing straight out of the front door is Earthly Branch VII or Wu. This means that the Mountain Direction is directly opposite, the Earthly Branch I or Tzu.

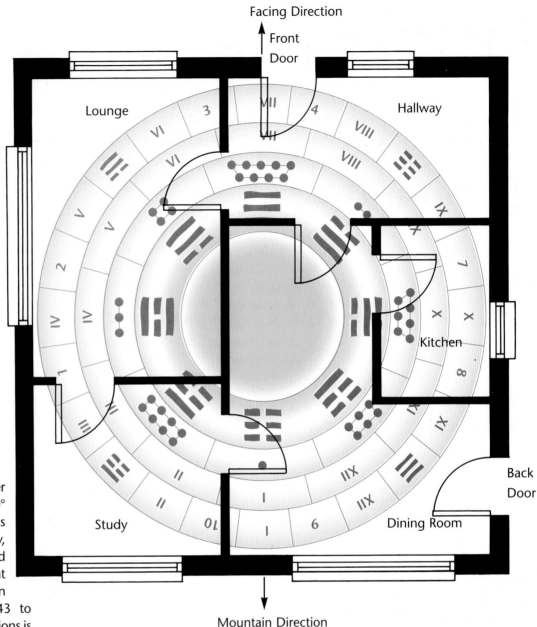

Facing Direction

Front Door

Lounge

Hallway

Kitchen

Back Door

Study

Dining Room

Mountain Direction

numbers of degrees. Remember that 0° (also 360°) is North, 90° is East, 180° is South and 270° is West. Stand inside the doorway, as far back as possible and sight directly out of the front door. Read off the degrees, then look up the table on page 43 to determine which of the 24 Directions is the Facing Direction. Each of the 24 Directions occupies 15°. Due magnetic North lies exactly in the centre of the Direction *tzu*. (Map North is not relevant).

Facing and Mountain Directions

Having identified the Facing Direction write it down in the box provided right. Then the direction of 180° that is pointing in exactly the opposite direction, known as the Mountain or Siting Direction, can also be read off. This pair of Directions, the Facing Direction and the Mountain Direction, are the characteristic Directions of the house.

Occasionally the building obviously faces a different Direction to that of its front door. For example, a flat might not have a front door which faces in the same Direction as the front door to the whole block of flats. In this instance both Directions should be checked. If you live in a flat and the front door of the building faces in a different Direction, or if the Facing Direction of your house is not the same as its front door Direction, you will need to take a second reading which will give you a second Facing and Mountain Direction.

> **WORKPOINT**
>
> *Enter here the Directions of your front door:*
>
> | | DEGREES | ONE OF THE 24 DIRECTIONS |
> |---|---|---|
> | Facing Direction | | |
> | Mountain Direction | | |

Your Sexagenary Year

Chinese time measurement is based on an uncomfortable mix of firstly the lunar calendar which dates back to the Emperor Huang Ti circa 2600 BC) and which is marked by the waxing and waning of the moon every 28-29 days, and secondly the need to accurately measure the sun's movement through the year and hence the seasons, based on 365.25 days per year.

The two heaviest planets in the solar system, Jupiter (shown here) and Saturn, take 60 years to return to the same position in relation to each other. Several scientists, such as John Gribben and Stephen Plagemann, have suggested that this 60 year cycle has a considerable effect on the biosphere of the Earth.

To avoid some of these problems, the yearly cycle in the Chinese calendar is known as the Sexagenary Cycle. This means a cycle of 60 and it consists of 60 days, 60 months or 60 years.

The Sexagenary Cycle does not fit into a year of 365.25 days, but then nothing divides neatly into this number. Therefore, five periods of 60 days plus 5 days over makes up one year.

The Sexagenary Cycle of 60 years is used to label each year with the same four characteristics. It is thought that people born in the same year of the Sexagenary Cycle will share certain characteristics.

Stems and Branches

The Sexagenary Cycle is made up by pairing together the 10 Heavenly Stems and 12 Earthly Branches (see pages 40-41). Those of you who are on the ball will notice that 10 x 12 does not make 60. Instead the Sexagenary Cycle is made by pairing 5 of the Stems with 12 of the Branches. The first year of the cycle is marked by the Stem *chia* and Branch *tzu* which when taken together make the year *chia-tzu*. *Chia-tzu* occurred in 1864, 1924 and again in 1985, each 60 years apart.

All this may sound a bit too technical, but we are just getting to the useful bit, which is where you identify the characteristics of your year of birth.

Elements and Animals

One of the 5 Elements is attached to each of the Sexagenary years. Much later one of the 12 Animal signs was attached to each year. The animal system although more popular is less specific because there will be, for example, 5 'years of the rat' in one 60 year cycle, but only one *chia-tzu* year.

Thus each year has its own Heavenly Stem, Earthly Branch, Element and Animal.

Working out your Sexagenary number

To determine your birth year's characteristics, let us start with the Sexagenary Cycle. To calculate which

Sexagenary character was active in your birth year simply deduct 3 from the full year, then divide by 60. The remainder (or 60) is the Sexagenary number. For example if you were born in 1963, subtract 3 to give 1960. Divide this by 60, round down the figure and multiply by 60. Subtract this figure from 1960 and you are left with a remainder of 40, which is your Sexagenary number.

From the Sexagenary number 40 you can calculate which Heavenly Stem and which Earthly Branch make up this Sexagenary combination. To work out the Heavenly Stem: keep subtracting 10 (the number of Heavenly Stems) from your Sexagenary number 40 until you have a remainder, which in this case is 10 (40-10-10-10= 10). The Heavenly Stem is therefore 10 *kuei*. To work out the Earthly Branch: keep subtracting 12 (the number of Earthly Branches) from your Sexagenary number 40 until you get a remainder, which in this case is 4 (40-12-12-12= 4). The Earthly Branch is therefore IV *mao*. The Sexagenary combination is therefore 10-IV or in Chinese *kuei mao*.

From page 40 you can see that Heavenly Stem 10 is attributed to the Element Water, while Earthly Branch *mao* is associated with the Rabbit. Hence anyone born in 1963 is a Water Rabbit.

THE CHINESE NEW YEAR

Before calculating your Sexagenary year of birth you must first establish your year of birth according to the Chinese calendar. In practice this step only affects those who were born between 1st January and 20th February (if you were not born during this time, simply ignore this step). If you were born in this part of the year before the Chinese New Year (which varies from year to year) you should subtract 1 from your year of birth. For example someone born on 14th January 1966 will use 1965 for these calculations because the Chinese year 1965 did not end until 20th January 1966.

There is no simple rule for determining when the Chinese New Year occurs, except that in this century it occurs between 20th January and 20th February on the first New Moon of the year.

The Tung Shu *or* Chinese Almanac *sells more than three million copies each year. It contains the calendar details for the coming year, including the date of the New Year and the auspicious Directions and days throughout the year for doing specific things. The Almanac also includes a host of other things, from weights and measures to rather rough pronunciation guides to English!*

WORKPOINT

Enter here the Sexagenary character of:

	NUMBER	STEM	BRANCH
Yourself			
Your partner			

WORKING OUT YOUR STEM, BRANCH AND SEXAGENARY COMBINATION

Find your Sexagenary Number

Take your year of Birth		1970
Minus 3		3 -
		1967
Divide the result by 60	$1967 \div 60 = 32.8$	
Round down the number		32
Multiply this number by 60	$32 \times 60 =$	1920 -
Subtract to get your Sexagenary number		**47**

Find your Heavenly Stem

Take your Sexagenary number (see left)   47

Keep subtracting 10 from it until you have a remainder:

$47 - 10 - 10 - 10 - 10 =$ **7**

This is your Heavenly Stem

Find your Earthly Branch

Take your Sexagenary number (see left)   47

Keep subtracting 12 from it until you have a remainder:

$47 - 12 - 12 - 12 =$ **11**

This is your Earthly Branch

If when subtracting your final figure is zero, your Sexagenary number is 60

Your Animal Birth Year & Element

The 12 Chinese animal 'signs' are familiar to almost everyone. In fact these relate directly to the 12 Earthly Branches (see pages 40-41). They are also allocated to the months of the year, and to years in a 12 year cycle.

YOUR SIGN & ELEMENT

How to work out your Sign
Take the last two digits from the year in which you were born. If the number is greater than 11, subtract 12 from it. Keep subtracting 12 until you have a number less than 12. Then read off your sign from the table below:

Animal Birth Year	
0	Rat
1	Ox
2	Tiger
3	Rabbit
4	Dragon
5	Snake
6	Horse
7	Goat (Sheep)
8	Monkey
9	Cock
10	Dog
11	Pig
12	Rat

How to work out your Element
To check the Element of your year of birth, keep subtracting 10 from the last two digits of your year of birth until you reach a number which is 10 or less, then read your Element off from the table below:

Element of Birth Year	
0	Metal
1	Metal
2	Water
3	Water
4	Wood
5	Wood
6	Fire
7	Fire
8	Earth
9	Earth
10	Metal

To work out which animal sign corresponds to your year of birth you must first adjust your year if you were born in the first two months of the year (see The Chinese New Year, page 49). Then working from your birth year you can determine your animal sign (see box, left).

The Chinese ideogram for the eighth animal sign can mean either a sheep or a goat. Interestingly the dragon is included as if it was real. It is possible that just as the lion has been mythologized by the Chinese, so the dragon is a memory of an animal which once walked the earth.

Relationships
In popular Chinese astrology the animal signs, or more correctly the 12 Earthly Branches, are used to determine compatibility between couples. The full Chinese horoscope however is made up of the details for the month, day and hour of birth as well as the year. This is, however, only the tip of the iceberg, because it is the much more subtle interplay of the resulting feng-shui luck and influences that derive from your time of birth which really effect a relationship.

PERFECT PARTNERS

The 12 animal 'signs' are allocated in order around the compass Directions, as well as to the months of the year. They are grouped together in four triplicities. Each group of three 'signs' will get on well with each other. The four groups are:

Rat   Dragon   Monkey

Ox   Snake   Cock

Tiger   Horse   Dog

Rabbit   Goat   Pig

OPPOSITES

People born in the year of 'signs' which are directly opposite each other however will clash. Any relationships between people of opposing 'signs' is bound to be a rocky one. These opposites, together with their compass Direction, are:

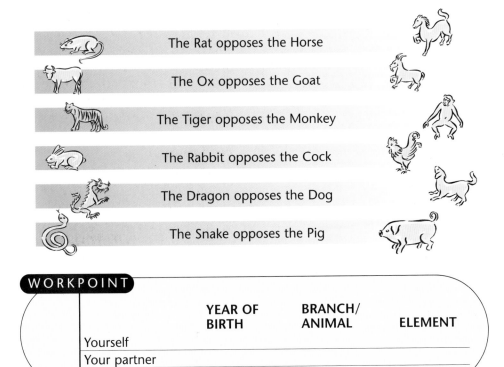

The Rat opposes the Horse

The Ox opposes the Goat

The Tiger opposes the Monkey

The Rabbit opposes the Cock

The Dragon opposes the Dog

The Snake opposes the Pig

WORKPOINT

	YEAR OF BIRTH	BRANCH/ ANIMAL	ELEMENT
Yourself			
Your partner			

CASE STUDY

James was born in 1958. To determine his Chinese animal 'sign' take '58 and continue taking 12 from it until you are left with a number less than 12, in this case 10. Reading from the table on the opposite page, 10 indicates that James's animal 'sign' is the Dog.

To calculate his corresponding Element, continue to subtract 10 from '58 until you are left with a number which is 10 or less, in this case a balance of 8. This number indicates that Earth is his Element.

As the animals are linked together in compatible groups (see table above) James can immediately deduce that he is likely to get along well with someone born in the year of the Tiger or the Horse.

FENG-SHUI

Calculating Your Personal Magic Number

To find your personal lucky and unlucky Directions, you must first calculate you own 'Kua number'. Technically this is the 'natal star' for your year of birth and part of Chinese Nine House Astrology.

Traditional feng-shui books provide tables and complicated calculations for deducing your Kua number, but the following explanation is a short cut. On pages 54-55 you will discover the significance of each of your best or worst Directions.

Working out your Kua number
The formula for calculating your Kua number differs according to whether you are a man or a woman. You should work out your Kua number and that of your partner, and make a note of it in the box provided on the opposite page as it will be useful to refer to in subsequent chapters.

First you must establish your year of birth according to the Chinese calendar. In practice this step only affects those who were born between 1st January and 20th February. If you were born in this part of the year before the Chinese New Year, you should subtract one from your year of birth (see page 49). If you were not born in January or early February, you simply ignore this step.

If you are a man, start the calculation by adding together the last two digits of the year of your

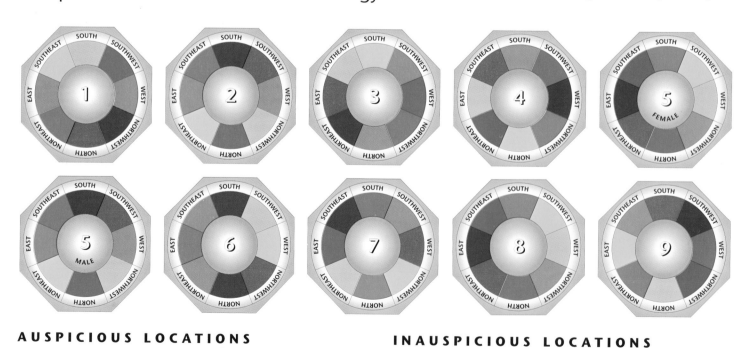

AUSPICIOUS LOCATIONS

■ mild good fortune   ■ health   ■ relationships & family   ■ great prosperity & success

INAUSPICIOUS LOCATIONS

■ accidents & frustrations   ■ mischief & quarrels   ■ bad fortune   ■ least fortune

birth. (If the total number is greater than 9, then add the two digits of the total number together). This will give you a single digit. Subtract this digit from 10. This is your Kua number.

The calculation for women is slightly more complicated than for men. If you are a woman, start the calculation by adding together the last two digits of the year of your birth. If the total number is greater than 9, then add the two digits of the total number together to give you a single digit. Add 5 to this digit. (If the total number is greater than 9, then add the two digits of the total number together.) The result is your Kua number.

Good and bad Directions

Once you have calculated your Kua number then look at the illustration of the Pa Kua (opposite page) for this number and you will see that your best Direction is shaded in yellow, with your other good but less important directions in orange and red. Your bad Directions are not all bad, but they are Directions which you should try not to emphasize. They are coloured with the cooler shades of the spectrum and your worst Direction is coloured with the darkest colour. To find out the exact meanings of these Directions and how to modify or emphasize them see pages 60-63.

From a practical point of view what you should aim to do, if you have the option or you are building a house completely from scratch, is to position unimportant rooms like storerooms or toilets in your worst Directions, with important rooms like your bedroom in your best sectors. At any rate you should make great efforts not to locate your front door or main bedroom in the less auspicious sectors, especially the very darkly coloured sector.

There are nine possible Kua numbers, with 5 having a different male/female interpretation. The warmest sectors are the most auspicious, while the coldest colours are the least auspicious.

CASE STUDY

1. Jill was born on 16th January 1962. To calculate her Kua number you first check if she was born before the Chinese New Year. This fell on 5th February in 1962, so her birthdate belongs in the previous year for the purpose of this short cut Kua number calculation. Hence her birth year was '1961'.

2. You must now add together the last two digits: 6 + 1 = 7

3. You should now check if your answer is greater than 9. It's not so there is no action on this step. (If it had been you would have had to add the constituent digits together.)

4. As Jill is a girl you must now add 5 to your answer: 7 + 5 = 12

5. Check if your answer is greater than 9. It is, so add its constituent digits together: 1 + 2 = 3

6. Jill's Kua number is 3.

To check Jill's partner Jack's Kua number you need his birthday, which is 22nd March 1948.

1. You must first check if he was born before the Chinese New Year. This fell on 10th February in 1948, so his birth year is unchanged.

2. You must now add together the last two digits: 4 + 8 = 12

3. You should now check if your answer is greater than 9. It is so you have to add the constituent digits together: 1 + 2 = 3

4. As Jack is a man you must now subtract your answer from 10: 10 - 3 = 7

5. Therefore, Jack's Kua number is 7.

Looking at the different Pa Kua for both of them it is immediately obvious that all of Jill's best Directions are in fact Jack's worst Directions, and vice versa. Thus Jill's best Direction is East (see the Pa Kua number 3), but for Jack East is inauspicious. This does not mean that Jack and Jill are incompatible, simply that if they live together they will have to compromise over which quarters to stimulate and which to leave dormant.

Had Jill's Pa Kua number been 2 whilst Jack's is 7, as you can see from the diagrams opposite, their best Directions would be an almost perfect match and their worst Directions could be mutually avoided. For example, Southwest is an excellent Direction for a Pa Kua 2 person, whilst it is also a good Direction for a type 7 person.

WORKPOINT

Enter here the Kua number of:

	KUA NUMBER	BEST DIRECTION (yellow sector)	WORST DIRECTION (dark green sector)
Yourself			
Your partner			

Are you an East or a West Group Person?

The division of people into East groups or West groups is a quick way to check feng-shui compatibilities. Using your Kua number (see pages 52-53), you can determine your Trigram, Element and group.

KUA NUMBER	TRIGRAM		ELEMENT	GROUP
1	K'an		Water	East
2	K'un		Earth	West
3	Chen		Wood	East
4	Sun		Wood	East
5 (for a man)	Ken		Earth	West
5 (for a woman)	K'un		Earth	West
6	Ch'ien		Metal	West
7	Tui		Metal	West
8	Ken		Earth	West
9	Li		Fire	East

If you are selecting a new house it helps to choose a house which is categorized as belonging to the same East or West group as yourself, which ensures that at least the basic house feng-shui will be in your favour. It is useful to know to which group your partner belongs. If they belong to the same group there is no problem, but if not, it is important to determine which of you is most sympatico with the house or flat you occupy.

Houses can also be categorized as East or West group houses. This does not just refer to the Direction in which they are orientated, but their suitability for East or West group people. Obviously a West group person will feel more at home in and have better feng-shui in a West group house. Similarly an East group person will feel at home in an East group house.

East houses

Houses are categorized as 'East Houses' if their front doors point in the Direction of the Elements Fire, Water and Wood, that is one of the following Directions:

Southeast, Northeast, Southwest or East.

West houses

The remaining houses are 'West Houses' and their front doors face Metal or Earth Directions, that is:

North, South, West, Northwest.

Your compatibility with your house

If your back door and front door do not face opposite Directions, then take the Direction opposite your back door as your 'front door' Direction for the purpose of this calculation.

Using your Kua number and the table to the left, check which group you and your partner belong to. Then check which group your current house belongs to, using the diagram on the opposite page.

EAST/WEST HOUSE POSITIONS

WEST HOUSES

In the diagram on the left houses with front doors facing North, South, West and Northwest are all West group houses.

EAST HOUSES

In the diagram on the right houses with front doors facing Southeast, Northeast, Southwest and East are all East group houses.

Write down the results in the Workpoint box, right. From this you can get a clear picture of the compatibility of your house and its occupants. Remember this is not a test of compatibility with your partner. East group and West group people can get along wonderfully well together. This is simply a test of your compatibility with your house.

What happens if one of you is compatible with the house and the other is not? Well in a perfect world you would each use a different front door and each have your own set of rooms, but in the real world you have to accept that the partner most compatible with the house is likely to get most benefit from the feng-shui. When planning locations of rooms for the other partner ensure that nothing too important is placed in their worst Directions.

SLEEPING PARTNERS

Relationships can be improved if partners sleep on the correct side of each other. The same applies to a lesser extent to the relative bed positions of other family members living in the same house, although it matters most with partners.

East group people should sleep on the positive side of West group people, that is to the Northwest, North, Northeast or East of them. This means that West group people must sleep on the negative side of East group people, to the Southeast, South, Southwest or West. For two people in the same group the sleeping position does not matter.

WORKPOINT

Enter here:

Are you an East or West group person? _____

Is your partner an East or West group person? _____

Is your house an East or West group house? _____

CHAPTER 6
THE FENG-SHUI OF YOUR HOME

Your Front Door

The front door to your house or flat is perhaps the most important feng-shui indicator and influence. It is like the mouth (or *kou*) of your dwelling and determines what *ch'i* is drawn into your home, whether positive or negative. If you live in a flat you should consider the door of your flat and the main door of the block of flats separately (see the case study on page 59).

The main door of your house should not open on to any obstruction like a high wall, a telegraph pole, a flyover or a source of 'secret arrows'. The main door should be solid and protective and not made of glass. It should not open into a narrow, dark or mean corridor, and it will be very constrictive to the entry of *ch'i* if the entrance hall has a beam in it.

Once the *ch'i* has entered the foyer, it circulates throughout the rest of the house. The arrangement of the corridors and stairs will then determine how the *ch'i* is distributed to the other rooms of the house. Ensure that corridors are well lit to keep the circulating *ch'i* 'bright'.

It is often said that stairs should not be directly aligned with the front door. This is a difficult precept to follow as many European houses, particularly terrace and semi-detached houses, are designed precisely like that. Stairs, of course, are just corridors in a different dimension. A curved stairway is fine, but a tightly-shaped corkscrew staircase will overagitate the flow of *ch'i*.

Favourable front door Directions
Ideally the front door should point in the most favourable Direction of the head of the household, and should not open on to an opposing blank wall or a major source of 'secret arrows' or on to the outer edge of a sharp bend in a road or watercourse. If any of the latter are unavoidable and cannot be blanked out, then maybe it is better to seal up the door and use the back door as your main house entrance, unless it is similarly afflicted.

Any of the Directions which are favourable to your Kua number (see pages 52-53) are good for your front door, but there is one special direction for each Kua number, called

A circular doorway into a traditional Chinese garden, allowing the entry of gently flowing ch'i.

the *sheng ch'i* Direction (colour-coded yellow in the illustration on page 52), which is best of all. See the box below for the best Direction for your specific Kua number (which you calculated on pages 52-53).

If you haven't got the perfect front door Direction, don't worry too much. Any of the red or orange Directions for your Kua number in the illustration on page 52 will do almost as well. At least you can check that *ch'i* entering the front door is beneficial. Stand on the threshold and look very carefully at everything you can see out of the door. Try to visibly block or deflect any obviously cutting *ch'i*. Make sure if you have a front garden that there is a gate shutting it off from the street. If the gate and front door can avoid being linked by a straight path from one to the other then so much the better.

Taking Form School feng-shui into account, there should be some small rise in front of the door such as a low garden wall. If the front area has been paved over by some previous owner or tenant, try to remove at least some of the paving slabs and plant an attractive plant or two, to bring life to the area.

The same rules apply to the front door of your office. It even applies to the front door of the building in which you work. If there are multiple entrances it is worthwhile using whichever entrance coincides with one of your good Directions (see page 52).

THE FRONT DOOR

NATAL STAR OR 'KUA NUMBER'	*SHENG CH'I* BEST FRONT DOOR DIRECTION
1	Southeast
2	Northeast
3	South
4	North
5 (for a man)	Northeast
5 (for a woman)	Southwest
6	West
7	Northwest
8	Southwest
9	East

FRONT DOOR DIRECTIONS

A tree 'threatens' the front doorway.

A stone statue which is too strongly Yang overpowers the doorway.

The bridge generates strong flows of cutting *ch'i* which strike the door. These are particularly strong as they have crossed water.

THE VIEW FROM YOUR FRONT DOOR

Negative: roof lines generate 'secret arrows' but not as strongly as a satellite dish.

Negative: the tree confronts the front door. This tree should ideally be screened by moving the gate entrance further along.

Negative: a satellite dish pointing directly at your front door is a strong source of 'secret arrows'.

Negative: a church spire generates 'secret arrows'.

Positive: a low wall in front of your door symbolizes the red phoenix.

Negative: the sharp points of a saw-tooth fence create 'secret arrows'.

Positive: a footstool or red phoenix formation in front of the door is good feng-shui. Ensure that any rocks used are smooth and don't form the shape of any potentially threatening creature.

Positive: a curving path to your gate is much better feng-shui than a straight, 'cutting' path.

Positive: a pond to one side of your front door is beneficial, although you should be careful about its exact position. Ponds are powerful feng-shui and side effects have been known.

Stagnant & Circulating *Ch'i*

After *ch'i* enters the front door it circulates rather as a wind would do, along corridors and through internal doors, passing out through windows.

A minimalist Japanese room allowing unimpeded ch'i flow. The Japanese have a similar, but not identical system to feng-shui.

Internal doors should be examined because if they line up in straight lines or open directly on to another from the front to the rear of the house, they will encourage *sha ch'i* to move too rapidly through the home. To modify this, some kind of barrier should be put in place between them. For example, in a long straight corridor from the front to the back of the house, the placement of a small table with flowers on it causes *ch'i* to deflect and beneficially go around the table rather than cutting straight through the room and escaping. Likewise internal doors directly opposite windows will encourage the loss of *ch'i*. Long corridors generally are a bad idea and are often the cause of problems in large offices, particularly those built in the 1950s and 60s.

Interior door alignments are most important as they are the access routes for *ch'i* from one room to another. If for example three doors align so that *ch'i* can whistle from one room to another, this rapid passage should be slowed down by hanging a wind-chime in its path. Likewise, misaligned doors that indirectly face each other should have mirror strips added to the apparently narrower of the two, to even out the apparent width of the doors.

CASE STUDY

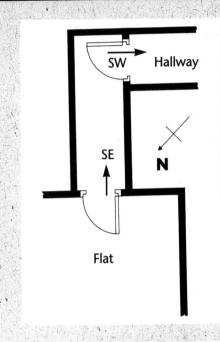

Nicola, who is a West group person with a Kua number of 7, lived in a flat whose main doors opened to the West on to a leafy well-protected street. Normally Northwest would be the best Direction for her, but West is almost ideal for her. However her individual flat door opened in a Southeasterly Direction on to a corridor which led off to the right.

For someone with a Kua number of 7, this is a bad Direction for a front door, a location called *lui sha* in Chinese which for Nicola meant missed opportunities at work, legal entanglements and accidents. In fact at the time of her feng-shui reading she had a court case pending over a motor accident and had just been passed over for promotion at work.

Her feng-shui practitioner advised her to alter the position of the front door to her flat, which is no easy thing to do. She went to see her landlord and eventually got his permission to enclose a section of the corridor that led to her flat. This meant that her outer door would now open on to communal areas in a Southwest Direction. Ten days later the case against her was withdrawn by the other side and life has improved for her in a number of other areas.

Minimizing clutter

One of the symptoms of stagnant *ch'i* is an accumulation of clutter and disorder. Traditionally the 'spring clean' is what sweeps all this away once a year. It is amazing how after such a spring clean you often feel so much better and more filled with optimism. But why confine this mood improvement to once a year? Try to keep clutter to a minimum at all times, because piles of unfinished work or unsorted rubbish act as a sort of mental break, subconsciously nagging away at the back of the mind and reducing your efficiency. When you are re-arranging furniture, consciously see if you can visualise the smooth flow of *ch'i* through the room. It should be able to curl sinuously through the room without having to break up on sharp surfaces or pool stagnantly in messy corners.

I am not talking purely of cleanliness, but of order and co-ordination. The Japanese, who also have a tradition akin to feng-shui, take austere purity to extremes in their minimalist decor. This is not essential for good feng-shui and as Western furnishings tend to be made

up of more pieces and more colours, the essence is to pursue balance and harmony. Any good interior decorator will know how to achieve this and to harmonize colours.

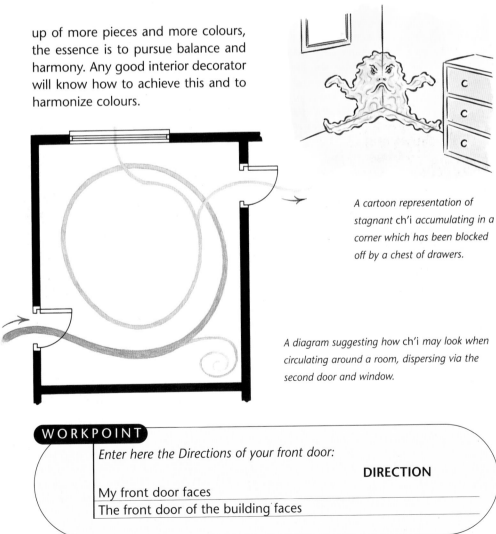

A cartoon representation of stagnant ch'i *accumulating in a corner which has been blocked off by a chest of drawers.*

A diagram suggesting how ch'i *may look when circulating around a room, dispersing via the second door and window.*

WORKPOINT

Enter here the Directions of your front door:

	DIRECTION
My front door faces	
The front door of the building faces	

Placement of Rooms Using the **Pa Kua**

It is important to evaluate the arrangement of the rooms in a flat or house. The positioning of frequently used rooms like the bedroom, living room and kitchen are most important, and need to be placed in good locations. Rooms like storerooms, unused bedrooms and toilets may be located in less auspicious parts of the house, although special consideration must be given to the toilet as its function involves the expulsion of water (*shui*) from the house.

The Pa Kua is the key to finding out which sectors of the house need stimulating in order to energize the various departments of your life. Techniques for stimulating the *ch'i* in specific corners are enumerated in chapter 9. For example if you are sitting examinations, then the corner to stimulate is the Northeastern corner which symbolizes education, while the Southwestern corner governs relationships and marital happiness. Conversely, if for example, the toilet is already located in this corner, you may be causing yourself unnecessary stress by symbolically 'flushing your marriage/relationship down the toilet'. This kind of symbolic thinking needs to be cultivated to give you a much better understanding of feng-shui.

The location of the toilet

Of course it is not always practical to cease using a toilet that is situated in a bad location. Instead the existence of the toilet could be disguised by keeping its door closed with a door-spring or locating a full length mirror on the door to make it 'disappear'. The mirror also prevents the loss of *ch'i* involved in the rapid movement of water down the toilet bowl, by reflecting it back into the house. If your house is made up of two storeys then you have to repeat the analysis of the location of the rooms separately for each floor.

It may seem strange that such actions should change the flow and concentrations of *ch'i*. At one level it may be that the action of making the changes in your environment impresses your subconscious with your positive decisions regarding that facet of your life. On the other hand the toilet is definitely an area of stagnant water and hence of stagnant *ch'i*, and this may well have a distinctly dampening effect on the sector of your life that the toilet is located in.

Analysing your home

Obviously you cannot move all the rooms of a house into favourable quarters. Nor can you re-build the house to conform with feng-shui rules, although some buildings including several major hotels have had extensive rebuilding for these very reasons. Having located clashes or trouble spots in the house it is often sufficient to apply one of the feng-shui formulae or cures listed in chapter 9. For example the addition of more or stronger lighting can increase the Yang quotient of an area. And the placing of mirrors can deflect 'secret arrows' or blank out undesirable areas of the house.

The whole house may be analysed by placing the Pa Kua (see pages 34–35) over the ground-plan of the house. After which you need to analyse the attributions of each room in terms of the corresponding sector of the Pa Kua.

After examining the house as a whole, each individual room should have the Pa Kua placed over its plan to decide which quarter or corner of the room corresponds with which Direction and hence which sphere of activity.

The essence of improving the feng-shui is to stimulate the appropriate sector to stimulate that type of luck. An L-shape house will have a corner missing, which will mean that the type of luck symbolized by that corner will be not taken into account.

USING THE PA KUA FOR ROOM PLACEMENT

YOUR LIVING ROOM

When applying the Pa Kua to the living room, make sure that the Trigram *li* points to the South.

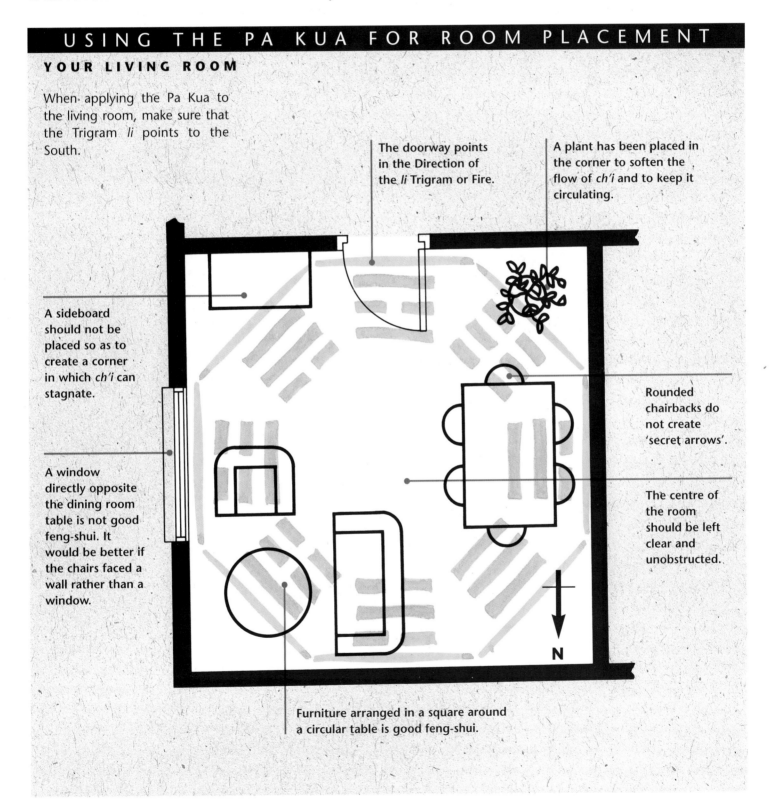

The doorway points in the Direction of the *li* Trigram or Fire.

A plant has been placed in the corner to soften the flow of *ch'i* and to keep it circulating.

A sideboard should not be placed so as to create a corner in which *ch'i* can stagnate.

A window directly opposite the dining room table is not good feng-shui. It would be better if the chairs faced a wall rather than a window.

Rounded chairbacks do not create 'secret arrows'.

The centre of the room should be left clear and unobstructed.

N

Furniture arranged in a square around a circular table is good feng-shui.

FENG-SHUI

The Eight Sectors of the **Pa Kua in** your Home

Having calculated your Kua number (see pages 52-53), now is the time to use it. Your whole house can be divided into eight sectors marked out by the eight Trigrams arranged in the Later Heaven Sequence.

LIFE ASPIRATIONS

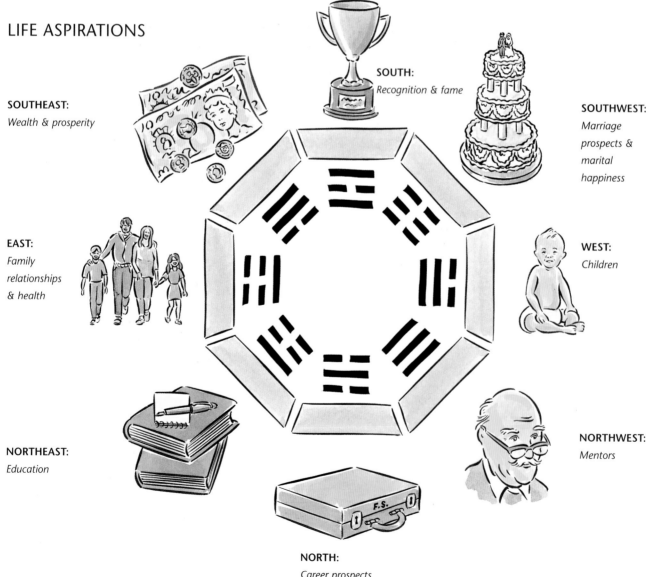

SOUTH:
Recognition & fame

SOUTHEAST:
Wealth & prosperity

SOUTHWEST:
Marriage prospects & marital happiness

EAST:
Family relationships & health

WEST:
Children

NORTHEAST:
Education

NORTHWEST:
Mentors

NORTH:
Career prospects

Each Trigram is associated with a particular aspect of life, for example career, children, health and so on. They are sometimes referred to as 'life aspirations'. By checking the associations of each Trigram against your home, you can establish which rooms (or corners of a room) correspond to which aspiration.

The Trigrams and the family

Each Trigram also traditionally has a member of the family asociated with it, but these should be taken symbolically rather than literally:

Li: Middle daughter
K'un: Mother
Tui: Youngest daughter
Ch'ien: Father
K'an: Middle son
Ken: Youngest son
Chen: Eldest son
Sun: Eldest daughter

For example, the Trigram K'un, which is made of three Yin or broken lines is associated with the mother and marriage and relationships. As the Trigram K'un is attributed to the Southwest, this is the sector which should be stimulated to improve your marital or relationship prospects.

THE EIGHT TRIGRAMS

TRIGRAM	DIRECTION/ ASPIRATION	ELEMENT
Li	South Recognition & fame	Fire
K'un	Southwest Marriage prospects & relationships	Earth
Tui	West Children	Lesser Metal
Ch'ien	Northwest Patronage	Metal
K'an	North Career prospects	Water
Ken	Northeast Education & learning	Lesser Earth
Chen	East Health & family relationships	Wood
Sun	Southeast Wealth	Lesser Wood

WORKPOINTS

Orientate a Later Heaven Sequence Pa Kua (see opposite) on the floor in the centre of your home. Use a compass to make sure that the Trigram *Ii* is pointed to the South. *Li* is the Trigram made up of a Yin (broken) line sandwiched between two Yang (whole) lines. Then visually sight each of the cardinal points, then the four intercardinal points, marking down the room that corresponds to each sector in the Workpoint box above.

A simple way of doing this is to draw a plan of your home, starting with the ground floor. Place the plan on a table so that it is aligned in the same Direction as your home, then place a compass on the plan, aligning the North-pointing needle with the North point on the compass. Use the compass to read off the basic Directions. Mark each room with a cardinal or intercardinal point. Using the ilustration on the opposite page

mark in the aspirations associated with each room. If your home is square or rectangular, or you live in a studio flat, then this procedure is straightforward. If the house plan is 'lumpy' then rule off the areas that jut out, such as balconies, and concentrate on the basic rectangle.

If your home is complex enough to have several wings then each of these should be considered separately, with the most emphasis placed on the part of the structure which contains the front door. Sometimes, where one room takes up the whole of one side of your home, then it might contain as many as three of the aspirations.

When this has been completed, repeat the same process for your bedroom, noting down which walls or corners correspond to which aspirations, so that you will know which areas to stimulate.

FENG-SHUI

Interior Decorating

Mirrors as a whole are favoured decorative feng-shui cures. They can act decoratively to mask an item which might otherwise generate bad feng-shui as ordinary mirrors can help move the *ch'i* around your home, or if used with the Pa Kua symbols painted around them they can be used to deflect incoming 'secret arrows' from outside the home.

Wind-chimes are useful for circulating ch'i and can be strategically placed to break up corridors or other straight alignments. Make sure that the pipes are hollow. A metal wind-chime can also be used to stimulate the Element Metal.

Bamboo flutes are wind (or feng*) instruments. They can be used to ease the flow of ch'i around obstructions like overhead beams.*

Overhead beams press down on the smooth flow of *ch'i* and are 'burdens' which 'press down' on luck. Beams over a dining table are considered particularly bad. To alleviate this problem, you should spotlight them (enhancing Yang energy) to 'lift' the oppression. Alternatively you should hang a traditional wind 'cure' such as a pair of flutes from them. Each flute should hang at an angle of 45° to the horizontal so that they appear to make up the Southwest and Southeast sides of the Pa Kua shape. The flutes act by conducting *ch'i* downwards and away from the area of congestion caused by the beam.

Square pillars, because they can send out 'cutting *ch'i*' in four Directions at once, need to be softened or disguised. One possible decoration is to train a climbing plant up them. Alternatively they could be made to 'disappear' altogether by facing them with mirrors. Converting them into a round column is another solution.

Colour

Colour plays an important part in both feng-shui and interior decorating within the home. The main purpose of adjusting the colours in a room is to balance the Yin and Yang elements, being careful to introduce at least 60% Yang for 40% Yin.

If an entire room is painted white and the furniture is cream, the overall effect may be very pleasing, but the Yin/Yang balance will not be satisfactory. Some darker Yin notes will have to be introduced to redress the balance.

Strong colours like red walls or furniture introduce Yang into the room. If it is necessary to introduce

COLOUR AROUND THE HOME

The basic Chinese interpretation of colour is symbolic. Each colour is also attributed to one of the five Elements. From the information given below it can be seen that the strongest feng-shui colours are red, green and gold which are used in the painting of the Pa Kua and many other Chinese decorations.

Red for happiness/festivity (Fire)

Green for peace and eternity, posterity and harmony (Wood)

White for peace, purity and sometimes mourning (Metal)

Gold for royalty, strength and wealth (also Metal)

Silver represents Metal

Yellow for gaiety (Earth)

Black for calamity (Water)

Blue for Heaven (dark blue also represents Water)

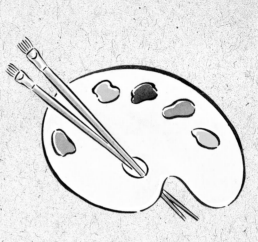

The feng-shui palette

ENHANCING FENG-SHUI IN YOUR HOME

A wooden Pa Kua with a mirrored centre (see below) should only be used outside the home to deflect 'secret arrows' or other threatening structures.

Inside the home feng-shui enhancers such as bamboo flutes may be hung strategically to enhance *ch'i* circulation.

Symbolically, it is sometimes useful to combine the shape of the Pa Kua by physically hanging a pair of bamboo flutes so that they form two of the slanting sides of an imaginary octagon (see right).

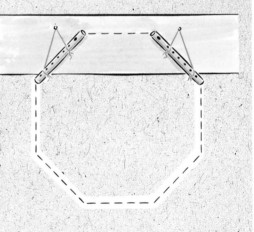

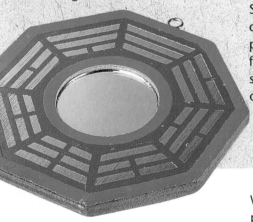

Yin highlights into a very male or Yang environment, then a selection of plants and flowers will soften the Yang and encourage the *ch'i* to meander and congregate.

Be careful that no wall colour confronts its own Direction, by that I mean that you should not paint a wall which faces West red because the symbolic colour of the West is red, nor should you paint a North-facing wall black, or a wall confronting a Wood Direction green and so on (see page 34 and the table above).

Colour can be provided more permanently by paint, or temporarily by coloured light bulbs which are useful to illuminate specific sectors. For example, your career could be stimulated by illuminating the North quarter with a blue bulb as the Element Water is associated in feng-shui with either dark blue or black.

Working out your keynote colour

To choose your best overall feature colour, check your birth year Element (see the Workpoints on pages 50-51) then select the Element that creates it (see The Production Cycle, page 37). Check these two Elements in the table above to determine your keynote colour. For example, if you were born in 1948, this is an Earth year. An appropriate Earth colour is yellow. Now you know that Fire creates Earth (from the Element Production Cycle on page 37), hence red is a good colour for you to use. Conversely, Wood destroys Earth, so excessive use of the colour green should be avoided.

Your Living & Dining Room

The living room and dining room, being the social centres of the house, should be designed with unity in mind. More than in any other room in the house, the flow of *ch'i* must be as uninterrupted as possible.

Traditionally, the best arrangement for living room furniture is one in which there are no sharp protuberances. Try to avoid L-shaped arrangements of chairs and sofas, as well as L-shaped rooms and L-shaped houses. The reason being that such a shape is incomplete and leaves a missing corner. As feng-shui is all about balance, this shape is undesirable.

The flow of *ch'i* through the room must be unhindered, with a smooth exit, perhaps through a second door. Furniture may be arranged in circular, square or octagonal (*pa kua*-shaped) groupings in the middle of the floor.

Arrange the furniture, especially chairs and the sofa, so that their backs do not face the doorway. Try to create a focus point. In earlier times, the fireplace would often have been the focal point. If your TV is currently the focus of attention, try to rearrange the room so the focus might be turned inwards on to a coffee table, with the TV placed off to one side.

Particular attention should be paid to furniture that is left out of these groupings and is lined up along the wall. Such items should be checked to see that they do not generate their own minor 'secret arrows' through being aligned with an open door, or with some part of the centre grouping. Corners should be occupied by enlivening items such as plants (only in the appropriate corner such as the Southwest) with a view to preventing the stagnation of *ch'i*.

Each window and door should be considered according to the direction of the inflowing *ch'i*. The *ch'i* should follow the lines of the furnishings in a spiral from room to room before it exhausts itself. The living room should not be cut off from the rest of the house in such a way that it can become a repository for stagnant *ch'i*. The converse of this is also true: a living room with too many doors is not only draughty but is liable to be a disperser of *ch'i*. Consideration should be given to sealing up one or two of the doors to such a living room.

It should also be easy to move around the living room without bumping into the corners of protruding furniture, for the flow of *ch'i* is very much like the movements of a dancer who will not perform well on a cluttered stage. Try to remove clutter from your living room, as the presence of clutter tends to lock up energy and prevent the free flow of *ch'i*.

Ideally, the living room should face South or one of your good Directions as indicated by your Kua number (see pages 52-53).

Dining rooms

If possible all dining chairs should back in the direction of a wall rather than a doorway. Neither the dining table nor any of the chairs should be positioned under an overhead beam. If this is unavoidable, then a false ceiling might be the best answer, as much as this might detract from the aesthetics of the room.

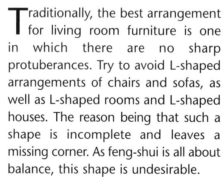

Good luck and good health are often symbolized by Chinese vases. The Dragon decoration symbolizes the flow of ch'i *through the earth.*

LIVING ROOMS WITH GOOD & BAD FENG-SHUI

SOME BAD POINTS

Overhead beams press down on the smooth flow of *ch'i* and are 'burdens' on posterity. Two bamboo flutes hung at 45° angles would conduct *ch'i* downwards and away from the area of congestion.

A living room with too many doorways is draughty and also disperses positive *ch'i*.

A bookcase is bad feng-shui as its sharp edges generate 'secret arrows' which are directed at anyone in its path. Position a climbing or trailing plant over it to combat this effect.

Too many dark colours and heavy furniture will effect the Yin/Yang harmony. A few lighter colours should be introduced to redress the balance.

Furniture should be arranged around a central focal point and should not point towards a doorway.

SOME GOOD POINTS

- Furniture should be arranged in a circular, square or octagonal grouping.

- Round tables are good feng-shui as positive *ch'i* is allowed to circulate.

- Plants soften the Yang and encourage positive *ch'i* to congregate and meander.

- Lots of light in a room promotes good energy.

風水 FENG-SHUI

Your Bedroom

The bedroom is perhaps the most significant room to examine after the positioning of the front door. After all, we spend about a third of our lives in our bedroom and so its feng-shui characteristics are obviously going to affect us deeply.

The location of the bedroom within the house is most important. The *Nien Yen* sector is the ideal location in the house for your bedroom (see table, below right). *Nien Yen* means 'longevity with descendants' and has a positive influence upon marital happiness. The *Nien Yen* sector is sand-coloured on page 52.

The position of your bed

Paying attention to the direction in which we sleep is one of the most important aspects of the layout of the bedroom. Many people have strong feelings about the direction in which they sleep, some finding one direction comfortable, and others finding the same direction uncomfortable and the apparent cause of restless nights. If practical, it is sometimes handy just to experiment with sleeping directions, if only to confirm for oneself the basic validity of this belief. Objectively it has been established that the direction of the earth's magnetic field definitely has an effect on the quality of sleep.

The head of your bed should be pointed in one of your four best Directions as determined by your Kua number (see pages 52-53) especially your *Nien Yen* direction (see table, below). The bed direction can affect all sorts of things including career, but obviously especially relationship and marriage luck.

Try to sleep with the head of the bed placed against a wall for support as this reinforces your sense of security. Headboards likewise help with this feeling of support in the same way that a mountain range situated behind a house gives it support. Insetting the bed into built-in constructions takes this rule to extremes and will in fact 'block' your potential.

Examples of bad feng-shui in the bedroom: a mirror directly reflecting the bed will contribute to disturbed nights; the metal bed frame will create 'secret arrows' aimed at the occupants; an overhanging and therefore threatening pair of pictures above the bed will subconsciously disturb the occupants; a heavy chandelier hanging directly above the bed will press down upon the occupants.

THE BEDROOM	
NATAL STAR OR 'KUA NUMBER'	*NIEN YEN* OR MAIN BEDROOM DIRECTIONS
1	South
2	Northwest
3	Southeast
4	East
5 (for a man)	Northwest
5 (for a woman)	West
6	Southwest
7	Northeast
8	West
9	North

Bad feng-shui for the bedroom

There are a few basic rules which should not be broken, the main one being that you should not sleep with your head pointed towards the door of the bedroom. This is because consciously or subconsciously there will always be a feeling of uneasiness about who might be entering the room if they cannot immediately be seen. This is a clear example of the overlap of feng-shui rules and ordinary commonsense. Make sure that you do not face the open door of an en-suite bathroom as the stagnant water-produced *ch'i* from here will weaken your *ch'i* accumulation.

Electric blankets, which cause you to sleep in a magnetic field, are definitely out. If you must use them, then use them to warm the bed first, then turn them off before getting into bed. Mirrors should be placed where they cannot be seen from the bed. The same applies to mirror tiles because they 'break up' the image, and therefore the relationship, reflected in them.

The bedroom should have only one entrance, so that the sleeper can absorb the accumulating *ch'i* rather than have it disperse rapidly out through a second doorway. The door of the bedroom should not open on to a stairwell or a kitchen as an undesirable rush of energy will come in through the door.

The bedroom should never be built over an empty space, a storeroom or a garage because it creates a *ch'i* vacuum underneath and adversely affects the occupants.

It is strongly recommended that you do not sleep in a room with an overhead beam, especially one that passes over the bed itself. The same rule applies to sloping, loft or A-frame ceilings which trap negative *ch'i* and pose a subconscious threat. Even the hanging of pictures or lights above your bedhead is not recommended as this leads to a subliminal feeling of threat, therefore reducing the quality of your sleep.

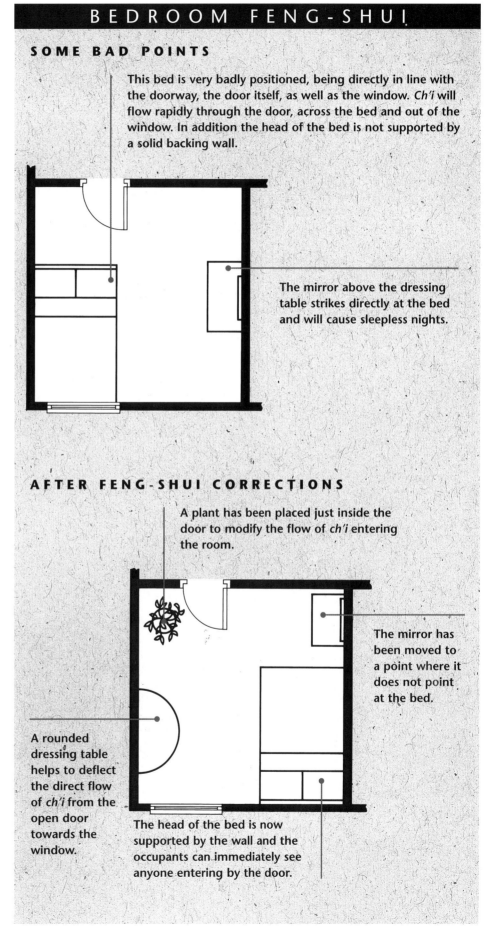

BEDROOM FENG-SHUI

SOME BAD POINTS

This bed is very badly positioned, being directly in line with the doorway, the door itself, as well as the window. *Ch'i* will flow rapidly through the door, across the bed and out of the window. In addition the head of the bed is not supported by a solid backing wall.

The mirror above the dressing table strikes directly at the bed and will cause sleepless nights.

AFTER FENG-SHUI CORRECTIONS

A plant has been placed just inside the door to modify the flow of *ch'i* entering the room.

The mirror has been moved to a point where it does not point at the bed.

A rounded dressing table helps to deflect the direct flow of *ch'i* from the open door towards the window.

The head of the bed is now supported by the wall and the occupants can immediately see anyone entering by the door.

Your Bathroom & Toilet

The location of your bathroom is not particularly critical, although the presence of running water in this room affects the water or *shui* balance of the house. Far more critical is the location of your toilet.

The toilet often tends to be in or adjacent to the bathroom and because it is from this room that water, and hence *ch'i*, is regularly and deliberately flushed away, the location is all-important. Even within a bathroom, toilets should if possible be aligned away from the bathroom door or hidden behind a half wall.

From a feng-shui point of view, whatever qualities are attributed to this sector will tend to get symbolically 'flushed away' because the toilet's watery connections act as a drain on *ch'i* accumulation. Toilets are also a strong generator of excess Yin and *sha ch'i*.

Accordingly, feng-shui practitioners always recommend that toilets are as unobtrusive as possible. Therefore the first feng-shui rule with regard to the toilet is always keep it closed: both the lid and the door. Put a spring-closer on the door if you can so that it closes even if you forget.

Fortunately, because of the nature of plumbing, toilets are seldom located at the centre of the house: if they were this would lend the character of excess Yin to the whole house.

Many of the precepts of feng-shui as applied to the toilet would delight the heart of a health inspector. For example, a toilet should not face directly towards the main entrance of a house. Also a ventilated lobby is desirable between the toilet and the rest of the house. However if your toilet is located in one of your most inauspicious Directions (see page 52), then the toilet will symbolically contribute to flushing away these bad influences. Armed with your Kua number, you can check if your toilet is well located (see table, opposite).

The position of the toilet should be carefully considered because the constant flushing of water disturbs the balance of ch'i in its vicinity. Here the householder has placed a screen in such a way that the toilet is not directly visible to anyone entering the room.

Flushing the toilet bowl is seen symbolically as flushing away accumulated water and therefore accumulated wealth.

CASE STUDY

Robert had a small business which was expanding. A much larger firm had a 25% share in the business and put a certain amount of business his way. After a year he moved to larger offices, where the unscreened hand basin and toilet were located in the Northwest sector. Soon after the move the larger firm withdrew its custom and offered to sell Robert their shares in the business. This was not totally unwelcome, but a surprise nevertheless until Robert remembered that the Northwest corner is the sector of patronage and helpful people. Hence the appearance of water being flushed away in this sector rapidly reduced the patronage of the larger firm.

Robert bought the shares back from the larger firm, but at the same time he made a point of reinforcing the Southeast corner of his office, the sector of wealth. One month later he made a business acquisition from the same company, which more than replaced the loss of their business and went on to earn him a considerable amount of money.

Bad toilet locations

Incidently the worst location for a toilet would be the locations listed on pages 56-57 as your ideal front door location. Toilets located in the Southeast, the wealth corner of the house, will certainly flush away your wealth almost as fast as it is created. If it is located in the Southwest corner of the house then marital problems are likely. Positioning the toilet in the North will delay your career prospects.

Having identified the toilet location and its likely effect on the feng-shui of the house, don't unnecessarily fret over a bad placement as this can be easily modified by feng-shui cures, more details of which can be found on pages 88-93.

THE TOILET

NATAL STAR OR 'KUA NUMBER'	BEST TOILET DIRECTIONS
1	Southwest, Northwest, Northeast
2	North, Southeast, South
3	West, Northwest, Northeast
4	Southwest, West, Northeast
5 (for a man)	North, Southeast, South
5 (for a woman)	North, East, Southeast
6	North, East, South
7	East, Southeast, South
8	North, East, Southeast
9	Southwest, West, Northwest

Your Kitchen

The kitchen is one of the most important rooms in the house and it is associated with the nourishment and health of the family. If the kitchen is located in an inappropriate position then illness and loss of livelihood can strike the occupants. The kitchen location also has health implications.

In many countries the kitchen is much more the social centre of the house than any other room. According to feng-shui principles, the kitchen door must be shielded away from direct access from the front door and should be in a position where the cook will not have his/her back to the door for too much of the time.

The structure of your kitchen is quite important. It should have a well-proportioned entrance door which allows the entry of *ch'i* and have a regular shape. The various facilities in a kitchen are easily assigned to their Elements. For example the stove or cooker is obviously a Fire item, whilst the fridge and sink are both attributed to Water. Ideally the Fire of the cooker should not be opposite and in confrontation with either of the Water facilities (the fridge and sink). The Direction that the cooker faces is the

Although superficially appealing, this galley kitchen has some serious feng-shui drawbacks. First there is an Element conflict between the Water of the sink and the opposing Fire of the stove. The positioning of the doors and windows means that 'secret arrows' can strike directly into the kitchen which should normally be the most protected part of the home.

most important factor. It must not directly face either the back or front doors if it is on the same floor as these doors, otherwise valuable *ch'i* will be lost. If the kitchen is not on the ground floor then this is not such a problem.

There is one special Direction, called the *T'ien Yi* direction, which is the best location in the house for your kitchen. If you can't simply re-orientate your kitchen, and few of us can, try to organise it so that the mouth of your stove, or at least the mouth of your microwave, points in this Direction. The importance of the oven mouth is that this provides nourishment to the family and therefore represents health and wealth. Depending upon your Kua number the best Directions are given in the table below.

As you should have already calculated your Kua number (see pages 52-53), you can check your kitchen immediately. Make sure that your oven mouth does not face any of your inauspicious Directions (see page 52).

The introduction of green into the kitchen, symbolizing Wood, helps to support both the Fire and Water Elements that make up the kitchen. The kitchen symbolizes everything from wealth to family bonds. As the rapid through movement of *ch'i* is bad feng-shui, try not to have windows or second doorways in line with the main door. Where the kitchen is part of the dining room as in a studio flat, provide a demarcation between the two.

THE KITCHEN

NATAL STAR OR 'KUA NUMBER'	T'IEN YI BEST OVEN DIRECTION
1	East
2	West
3	North
4	South
5 (for a man)	West
5 (for a woman)	Northwest
6	Northeast
7	Southwest
8	Northwest
9	Southeast

KITCHEN FENG-SHUI

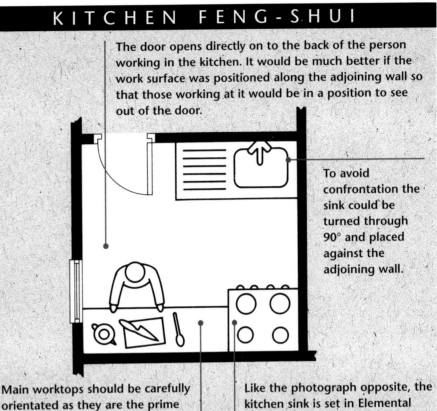

The door opens directly on to the back of the person working in the kitchen. It would be much better if the work surface was positioned along the adjoining wall so that those working at it would be in a position to see out of the door.

To avoid confrontation the sink could be turned through 90° and placed against the adjoining wall.

Main worktops should be carefully orientated as they are the prime working position in the kitchen.

Like the photograph opposite, the kitchen sink is set in Elemental opposition (Water versus Fire) against the stove.

CASE STUDY

Lucy had just had her kitchen totally redesigned by a firm of kitchen designers. This meant that her old stove whose mouth originally pointed in a Northeast Direction was replaced by one pointing towards the North, whilst her new refrigerator took the place of her old stove. She was very pleased with the improvements, but within three weeks things started to go wrong. Her finances, already strained by the new kitchen, took a turn for the worse and she lost a major freelance job which she had been relying on, through no fault of her own, and she also developed an unshakeable bout of 'flu.

Instead of consulting a feng-shui practitioner she set about calculating her Kua number (see pages 52-53). Having been born in

1973 she soon discovered that her Kua number was 6. Consulting a feng-shui manual she discovered that the stove used to face her *T'ien yi* sector, normally very favourable, but had been moved to face her *Lui sha* sector, which means in Chinese 'six killings', a rather dramatic expression of how she had been feeling.

Lucy immediately arranged to have the position of her refrigerator and stove switched and determined not to make such radical changes again without first checking her Directions. Her 'flu cleared up several days later, and a new job offer arrived in the post soon after.

Garden Paths & Alignments

Although there are many things you can do to improve the feng-shui of your home, there are still certain limitations. You cannot, for example, easily change the position of the front door, or the position of main walls. In the garden, however, you have much greater freedom to change things and configure your own feng-shui environment.

The essence of enhancing feng-shui is to balance the Yin and the Yang in the garden so that *ch'i* is encouraged to flow in a lazy, meandering fashion and to accumulate. Thus the presence of soft Yin foliage can be countered with the Yang of polished stones or boulders. Many of the principles that apply to the creation of Japanese gardens can be modified to produce a peaceful yet invigorating garden environment.

Designing your garden

The design of the garden should not be flat and lifeless or a basic rectangular shape where every part can be seen immediately upon entering the garden. If your garden is laid out in a rectangular fashion then maybe the introduction of a little imagination to give it more natural lines could work wonders. Try to introduce curving paths and planting

This garden shows a naturalistic approach with curved paths, a mature pond and well-screened peripheral boundaries.

patterns which lead the eye into the middle distance, but don't reveal the whole garden. Both these objectives can be achieved with a curving path apparently disappearing behind a screen of plants. A good mix of Yin and Yang, of colours, plants and different levels in your garden will enhance the feng-shui of your home.

Walls and fences

These can either let in or keep out surrounding feng-shui influences. They are very important as screens to block 'secret arrows'. So first of all walk carefully around your garden noting what you can see over the fences from every part of the garden. You should add additional trellis work to the top of fences to block out views of 'cutting' shapes, such as the intrusive lines of telegraph poles. By growing a vine over the trellis you soften or remove the cutting *ch'i* generated by that shape. Where the view is beneficial, the opposite holds true, and often a good outlook can be brought into your garden by constructing round 'portholes' in the walls if they are made of brick or simply lowering the height of a fence.

Try to encourage or locate strongly growing plants next to your walls and fences: this helps to modify the stark Yangness of the fence with the soft Yin of the foliage.

Paths and garden edging

These are important elements in the overall feng-shui environment of the garden. Try to visualise these as if they were streams and see where their natural flow leads. If garden edging runs in straight lines alongside rectangular beds then this will create 'secret arrows' and become a source of undesirable *sha*. If both paths and edging are laid out in curves they can take the place of streams and actually help to accumulate *ch'i*. If paths and edging are used in this way, thought has to be given to where they terminate. A

path might start at the back door and lead to a pond – such a path would be beneficial if curved. But a path that simply ran at right angles towards a fence at the end of the garden would not be beneficial.

Garden edging performs a similar task in conducting *ch'i*. If edging is to properly conduct the flow of *ch'i* it is important that loose earth or plants must not be prevented from covering the edging or blurring its definition.

A WELL-PLANNED GARDEN

The path flows in a curved, meandering fashion through the garden, much like a stream. Plants cloak the harsh fence lines and the pond helps to accumulate *ch'i*. Advanced feng-shui has much to say about the exact positioning of ponds and watercourses. The round table and round-backed chairs deflect *sha ch'i*. The large stone ornament introduces a touch of Yang to the garden to balance the Yin foliage and plants.

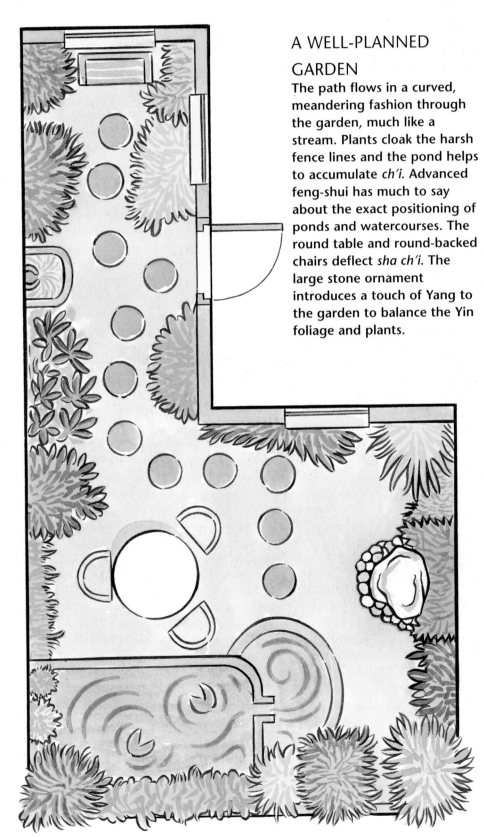

The Water Dragon: Streams & Ponds

Water is at the very heart of feng-shui, being 'shui', one of the two parts of feng-shui. Water is a carrier of *ch'i*, therefore wherever water accumulates, so *ch'i* accumulates, where water flows freely so *ch'i* flows freely, but wherever water stagnates so *ch'i* stagnates.

Ponds are great accumulators of beneficial ch'i. Ensure that the pond is surrounded by lush green foliage which help to balance the Ying/Yang elements.

A visibly flowing current which swirls and dimples on the surface of water is referred to as a Water Dragon. This flow of water, known as the movement of the Water Dragon, is the subject of many very complex and often secret Chinese texts. You can, if you are ambitious, 'build' a simple Water Dragon in your own garden by adding a fountain, pond or small stream. Flowing water is much more powerful as a collector and disperser of *ch'i* than any of the many complex compass formulae for calculating beneficial Directions.

Pools, streams and fountains

A curving stream, perhaps fed by a fountain, is an ideal addition to a garden. Even a very small and otherwise cramped back garden can benefit from a small electric pump-fed fountain, which is quite cheap to buy. The pump could even be set on a timer so that the fountain starts to flow in the early morning and again in the evening, rather than running all day.

Remember that stagnant water causes stagnant *ch'i*, so you must be sure to maintain the quality of water not only in your fountain or pool but even in your ordinary household drains. You can take care of the pool or pond with a block of slowly dissolving pond cleaner, available from most aquarium shops. Likewise, never allow the household drains to become blocked or clogged with leaves. Ensure that at all times the drains are clear, emit no foul odour and flow steadily.

The directional flow of water

A garden is an excellent place to experiment with Form School feng-shui, but be careful, some of the most powerful feng-shui formulae relate to the effects of the Water Dragon.

Like the rest of feng-shui, direction is of critical importance, particularly the visible direction that water enters or leaves your property. One of the

GARDENS WITH GOOD & BAD FENG-SHUI

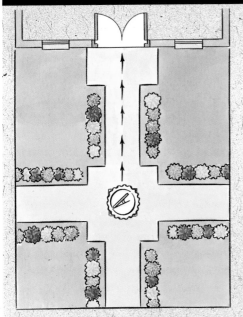

Ensure that your stream is regularly cleared of any debris which may generate *sha*.

The sinuous curves of the stream allow beneficial *ch'i* to meander around the garden.

The formal garden (above) contains a very structured design made up of straight lines. These generate 'secret arrows' which are directed towards the main door of the house.

The more aesthetic garden (right) is curved and meandering which allows beneficial *ch'i* to accumulate. The stream winds sinuously around the garden and is surrounded by healthy plants and foliage. This combination produces a peaceful yet invigorating environment.

The garden path follows the curve of the stream so that there are no sharp angles which would generate any cutting *sha ch'i*.

simplest rules to follow is to ensure these directions coincide with your own auspicious Directions (see page 52). Here Compass School feng-shui meets with Form School feng-shui in determining the correct Directions.

Make sure that water does not rush along in straight lines, taking with it the beneficial *ch'i*, but ensure it meanders in such a way as to accumulate the *ch'i*. It is particularly important to check the Direction of the flow of any water passing in front of the front door. If your house has its

front door facing one of the cardinal points, North, South, East or West, then ideally the water should flow from left to right as you look out of your front door. For front doors facing intercardinal points, the flow of water should be from right to left.

Ponds

Traditionally garden ponds have contained carp, koi or goldfish. The best combination of fish is supposed to be eight red or golden fish plus one black fish for balance, or if the

pond is not large enough for this then any odd number of fish. In particular, avoid having just four fish in a pond.

Rectangular ponds or those with long, straight sides or sharp angles are less auspicious and more likely to introduce *sha*.

In addition, natural water or water drawn from a natural stream, spring, well or water butt, is considered to be superior to the de-natured, chlorinated and disinfected water supplied by tap in many cities.

Perfect Plants, Soils, Shade & Sun

Vegetation is associated with the life force, *ch'i*.

Therefore areas that cannot support vegetation are

dead or at least lack *ch'i* energy.

Newly developed housing estates tend to be barren of *ch'i* because the soil has recently been cut and dug during the process of building the houses. If a site is exposed, without vegetation, then it is vulnerable to rough winds which disperse the *ch'i*, rather than accumulating it. Traditionally, evergreens are better for accumulating *ch'i* as they are symbolic of longevity because they do not shed their leaves during winter. The best plants from a feng-shui perspective are those with profuse foliage, flowers or fruit and those which are long-lived. Plants generally, if they are not spikey, are softeners of the landcape and trap gentle breezes. Even a spikey plant like a strelitzia (bird-of-paradise plant) can add a useful touch of Yang to a garden.

Water, light and shade

Gardeners have long recognised the effect that varying mixes of light or shade have on the growth of certain plants. Some are naturally Yin plants and grow in the shade, examples of these types of plants are ferns such as *Asplenium scolopendrium*, hostas, hellebore and woodland cyclamen.

Others are Yang plants and demand strong sunlight. Plants like bamboo might be placed along the Northern fence of a garden belonging to an East-West orientated house, so that they get the maximum sunlight and provide useful screens. The reverse is true in the Southern hemisphere where the warmest corners of the garden will be North-facing.

Similarly, every gardener knows where the dampest, even most waterlogged corners of the garden are situated and these areas are suitable for Yin plants. Flourishing plants are not just a sign of good gardening but also of flourishing *ch'i*. A harmonious mixture of Yin and Yang plants is recommended.

The Strelitzia *is a strongly coloured and spikey Yang plant which can be used to advantage to stimulate Yin areas in the garden.*

Hostas form a perfect transition between the flat earth and the overhanging vegetation. Hostas grow well in shady conditions while the colourful geraniums prefer a lighter spot. A perfect Yin-Yang combination.

Types of soil

Soil types play a part in feng-shui and traditional texts recommend prevention against stagnant or 'rotting' or termite-infested soils as they are symptomatic of stagnant *ch'i*. Such areas, if they cannot be avoided, need to be well turned over and aerated, and then stabilized with the addition of something like good clean river sand.

Good and bad feng-shui

Another thing to avoid in the garden is leaving rotting or dead plants or grass cuttings in place as they generate too much Yin energy. The remains of a tree stump rotting in the ground is even worse as it attracts stagnant *ch'i* as well as insects. Such tree stumps should be totally rooted out. In fact one of the worst feng-shui situations is that of a house built over a buried tree stump, or a closed-up well. The *sha ch'i* generated under these circumstances will overwhelm the occupants of the house.

It is beneficial to cover freshly dug earth wherever possible, as a newly dug bed implies a recently cut 'dragon'. This principle also extends to the transition between soil and plants. In Japan the *Acer* with its autumnal colours is often used as a transitional plant between the bare soil and the greener neighbouring plants. Other transitional plants which should be placed at the edges of ponds to hide the sharp transition between water and earth include the gunnera. Ivy and creeping plants help to soften the harsh outlines of buildings and may be useful in covering sharp or pointed structures.

Trees and ponds are the most natural elements of urban feng-shui practice. Pine is often picked out as a single feng-shui tree. In a Chinese setting such trees are often a centre for food offerings. From a feng-shui point of view they form an energy focus for a garden.

FENG-SHUI

The **Perfect** Garden

There is much scope for increasing the beneficial *ch'i*-accumulating abilities of the garden landscape. It is in fact this premise which led to the creation of the exquisite Zen gardens located around many shrines in China and Japan. The manipulation of the existing elements of the landscape into these gardens, where nature is enhanced not uprooted, is a specialized application of feng-shui.

For centuries the garden has played a very significant role in Chinese life both at Imperial level and in the compounds of ordinary people.

When putting together your own garden, make sure no one feature dominates the garden as balance is very important. The addition of hard landscaping such as smooth rocks or stones helps to introduce Yang into what might otherwise have been a very Yin garden. Areas of raked gravel also produce textural differences in a garden. These can be carefully selected for colour as well as texture.

Be careful though when you introduce more characterful rocks. These can often take the shape of some creature which is unfavourable to the garden and its occupants, and will generate *sha*. One such naturally occurring rock in Hong Kong was seen by the local feng-shui practitioner as a huge frog gulping up its surroundings. It may well have been coincidence, but soon after

Traditional Japanese or Chinese gardens often have symmetrically curving raked gravel areas, representing the water-like flow of ch'i through the land. The stone lantern takes the place of a pagoda on a small scale, anchoring the ch'i energies.

developers built flats nearby, there was a massive landslip and the mudflow literally swallowed the building with considerable loss of life. Even on a small scale it pays to be careful with such rocks!

Rockeries and pagodas

A garden on the North side of the house could benefit by having a rockery sited against the Northern wall, offering support to the house as a rockery represents *shan* or the mountains. However, make sure it does not directly confront the back door. In large formal Chinese gardens, particularly if exposed, pagodas are often placed in the Northeast or Southwest directions to earth the atmospheric *ch'i*. In a small garden, porcelain miniature pagodas could be placed in the same locations. A pagoda does not have to be the oriental equivalent of a garden gnome!

Water features

A pond or stream represent *shui* or water. If there isn't a rockery, then you might consider building a small island in the pond. The positioning of the water features in the garden are extremely important. Ideally the pond should be placed in front of the house to the South. However many Western-style houses have little space in front and will often find it more convenient to site the pool in the back yard or garden. Professional feng-shui advice might be worthwhile obtaining for the siting of a large or complex pool.

L-shaped houses

If you already have, or are thinking of building a garden room or conservatory, you should take advantage of this to fill in any 'missing corners' of your house. If your house is already rectangular, try not to create a 'missing corner' by building a conservatory along part of one wall only. Try to build along a complete wall so that the rectangularity of your house is not destroyed.

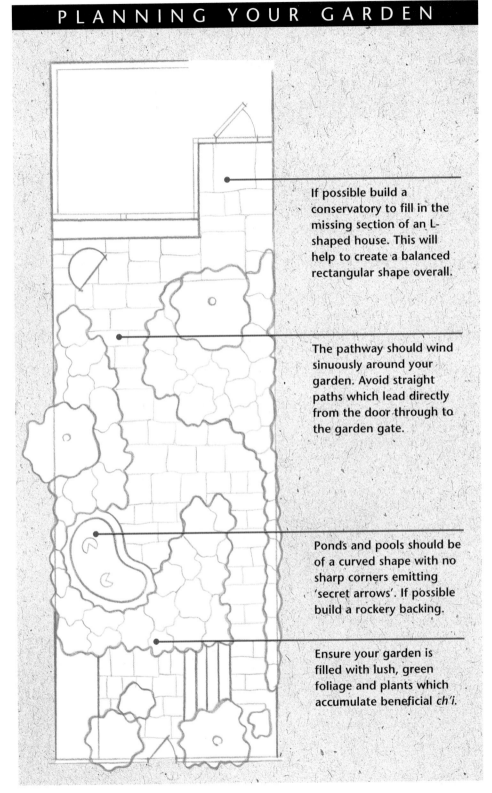

If possible build a conservatory to fill in the missing section of an L-shaped house. This will help to create a balanced rectangular shape overall.

The pathway should wind sinuously around your garden. Avoid straight paths which lead directly from the door through to the garden gate.

Ponds and pools should be of a curved shape with no sharp corners emitting 'secret arrows'. If possible build a rockery backing.

Ensure your garden is filled with lush, green foliage and plants which accumulate beneficial *ch'i*.

Enhancing sectors of your garden

To determine what parts of the garden need special attention simply apply the Pa Kua figure (see pages 34-35) to the garden, marking out appropriate sectors. For example, to stimulate career prospects, add Water or Water-creating Elements to the Northern quarter. Set up garden lights in specific corners of your garden. Stimulating the Southwestern corner, for example, can bring significant gains in the marital and relationship spheres of your life.

CHAPTER 9
CURES FOR SPECIFIC PROBLEMS

Improving your Relationships

In the area of relationships, feng-shui can cause problems as well as solve them. For example, if the husband is an East group person and the wife is a West group person, some compromise will need to be made as to whose best Directions prevail.

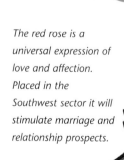

The Chinese character for 'bliss' doubled to represent a felicitous relationship.

The red rose is a universal expression of love and affection. Placed in the Southwest sector it will stimulate marriage and relationship prospects.

Although fate, or Heaven luck as the Chinese put it, may govern your opportunities for meeting suitable life partners, feng-shui certainly has a strong influence on how these relationships turn out. When moving in with someone, often the nature of a relationship will change in totally unexpected ways, and not just those associated with learning to live in close proximity with a new person. If you are the person doing the moving, areas of your life, such as career or patronage, might suddenly change for no apparent reason. The answer of course is that the movers feng-shui environment has changed totally, whilst the partner whose flat or home it was originally will still have the same feng-shui conditions. If both partners move into a totally new home, then both may be affected.

Important feng-shui factors

Feng-shui practitioners claim that if the partnership feng-shui is correctly positioned and stimulated then the chances of either partner wishing to embark on an outside relationship is fairly limited.

One of the classic stimulators of ch'i is the fish tank or fountain. Some feng-shui practitioners advise the setting up of such a tank near the main door of the house. However if this is placed on the right-hand side of the main door, looking out, it can increase the sort of ch'i which attracts other women to the husband, a development which will not be conducive to a happy marriage. It is for reasons like this that feng-shui manipulation can not only solve, but can also create problems. A good feng-shui adviser should however be able to avoid these pitfalls. The key features are not surprisingly:

• the location and layout of the bedroom
• the relative sleeping positions of the couple
• the Southwest sector of the bedroom – the sector of relationships and marriage
• your personal *Nien Yen* direction (see pages 68-69)
• if there are children, then the West and East sectors of the house are also important because the behaviour of children often affects a relationship. The East is the sector of family relationships.

Bad feng-shui in the bedroom

In the bedroom make sure that a mirror does not reflect the bed, thereby creating a double image of the marriage. Despite the swinging sixties, a ceiling mirror is also not a good idea!

It is important to guard against destructive feng-shui features in the Southwest sector. Any windows should be carefully checked to see that there are no 'secret arrows' or sharp cutting edges directly pointing towards the home. Try not to choose a house or flat with water function rooms like a kitchen or bathroom in the Southwest sector. The flushing of a toilet in this sector will repeatedly disturb the *shui* (water) balance, resulting in turbulence in the marriage and dispersal of its special qualities. The solution to this is either to use a different toilet in the house, or to ensure that the room is disguised as much as possible with curtains or a full length mirror.

Good feng-shui in the bedroom

Techniques for beneficially stimulating the *ch'i* are explained on pages 88-93, but the use of traditional romance symbols such as red roses in the Southwest sector is beneficial. From Chapter 3 you will remember that red is symbolic of Fire and Fire produces Earth. The Southwest sector is the Earth sector, so the use of the colour red will help 'produce' more Earth and stimulate this sector. If you follow the last sentence then you are well on your way to instinctively grasping the basis of feng-shui. It follows that red lights or anything red, particularly in pairs, is useful.

The best location for the bedroom

Your personal Pa Kua number was calculated on pages 52-53. Look back and remind yourself of your Natal star Kua number. On pages 68-69 you discovered your *Nien Yen* or relationships Direction.

Provided there are no other counter indications, the *Nien Yen* sector is an excellent one for siting the master bedroom, or if that is not possible, then sleep with your head facing this Direction inside the existing master bedroom. Obviously both partners may have different *Nien Yen*

Directions. In which case select either your Direction or if you are reading this book together, then your wife or girlfriend's Direction.

Children's bedrooms

Children can sometimes place an intolerable strain on a marriage, and so stimulation of the good feng-shui

qualities of the West sector and an analysis of the feng-shui of the children's bedroom can often reduce the amount of inter-generational discord, thereby allowing the relationship between the couple to continue flowering. Likewise the East, the sector of family relationships, could benefit from mild stimulation.

Even the best relationships can benefit from direct feng-shui stimulation.

Get that Job: Energizing your Career

By now you should know that the first thing to check when analysing the effect of the feng-shui of your home on your job or career is the appropriate sector according to the Pa Kua. This of course is the North sector, complemented partly by the fame and recognition sector in the South of your home.

The iron horseshoe is a traditional Western symbol of luck which can be used (in the upward position) to stimulate good luck. it is particularly useful in a sector where the Element Metal prevails, such as the West or Northwest.

To create opportunities for career advancement, first carefully analyse the external influences impinging on the Northern side of your home. Check all windows pointing in this direction for visible 'secret arrows'. Any invisible 'secret arrows' which are screened off so you cannot see them do not have an effect.

Stimulating your career sector

If career is your priority, ahead of say family or education, then plan to stimulate this Northern sector. Look again at the Pa Kua and identify its Element, which is Water. What produces Water? Look at the Production Cycle on pages 36-37, and you will see that Metal produces Water. Now think laterally about appropriate symbols. One that comes to mind is the horseshoe, a traditional Western symbol of luck, and made of Metal. Remember however, if you use this, position it so that its 'horns' point upwards so that the 'luck does not run out'. Don't think of this chain of associations as thinking superstitiously, but as thinking symbolically. Another suitable Metal *ch'i* enhancer is a metal wind-chime. Make sure however that the wind-chimes are of the hollow sort, not solid metal.

Make sure that you don't over-emphasize the Element Earth in the Northern quarter by displaying crystals or other Earth-oriented objects. This is because Earth destroys Water and that is the reverse of what you wish to happen in the Northerly career sector.

As the colour of Water in the North is either dark blue or black, another symbolic addition to this corner is a blue light. A fish tank directly symbolizing Water is good, but you should choose black or dark blue fish, rather than too many gold or red fish.

Thinking through the Production Cycle of the Elements (see pages 36-37), it should be obvious that as Wood is produced by Water, Wood must therefore exhaust Water in this production. Placing indoor plants in the Northern sector of the house is not a good idea as they will sap or reduce the vitality of Water in this particular sector. Another career-related consideration is the direction in which the windows open. Inward-opening windows are considered harmful to careers.

Feng-shui in the office

At your place of work, when you have meetings that are important to your business, try to position yourself at the conference table so that you do not have your back to the doorway. If possible you should try to sit facing one of your best Directions (see page 52).

Feng-shui is just as applicable in the work environment as it is in the home. After all we spend most of our life either in bed or work! It is important that the workspace environment is laid out in such a way that colleagues get on with each other, otherwise friction very easily develops.

You can of course treat your office in the same way as you have checked the feng-shui of your home. Careful placement of your desk is of prime importance. Using indoor plants placed to soften the flow of *ch'i* through the door should improve the feng-shui of your office. Use your Kua number to determine the very best Direction to face whilst working at your desk. Make sure however that the door is not positioned directly behind you.

ENHANCING YOUR CAREER

A goldfish bowl placed in the Northern quarter symbolizes and strengthens the Water Element. North is the career sector which corresponds to Water.

Business & Office Feng-shui

Feng-shui in the business environment is almost as important as in your home. Perhaps the most important consideration is to try and protect your back so that you don't back on to either an open door, a window or other desks if you can help it. You should try to place your desk in a 'commanding position'. It should not be pointed directly at colleagues because this could engender a feeling of unconscious hostility.

If you are lucky enough to have your own office then its entrance door should be located in one of your auspicious Directions (see table, opposite).

The area around your immediate working area should be free of clutter, especially at floor level, where it is useful to group together trailing wires so that they don't form a criss-cross of conflicting lines and energies.

Desk areas

On the desk surfaces, clutter is sometimes impossible to avoid, but you should try to prevent the accumulation of semi-permanent piles of paper. Even if your in-tray is full, you should try to go through it at least once every few days. Any pile of papers that is unconsulted regularly will accumulate stagnant *ch'i* and should instead be filed and then retrieved when needed. If you have an office to yourself then you can get to work on the Northern sector to enhance your career and the Southeast sector to enhance your wealth, which in a work environment leads to a pay rise.

Try to avoid sharply angled desk lights – a curved neck 'banker's lamp' is better. Bookshelves if tidy are not too much of a problem, but if the shelf edges look like they might generate cutting *sha*, then fixing doors to enclose them will improve the situation.

Feng-shui can improve staff relationships and foster a better working atmosphere in your office. In this way it is invaluable, so look carefully at the situation of individual staff desks.

Entrances and reception areas

When a business relies upon customers, the attractiveness of the entrance cannot be over-stressed. Although the customer should be able to see in, he or she should not be able to see all of the shop. In an office, the reception area just inside a door should not be cluttered with packages awaiting collection. Any alignment which poses a 'secret arrow' threat to the entrance should be blocked or deflected if possible. Rows of indoor plants are useful for this and to screen workers from direct alignment or having their backs to doorways, even internal ones.

Enhancing the wealth sector

Obviously for a business the Southeast sector, the wealth sector, is the relevant one. Here the Element is Wood and as you know from the Production Cycle of the Elements, Wood is produced by Water. A fountain or fish pond in this sector will enhance the wealth creating potential of the business. However be careful, for the wealth created goes to the business and its owners, not necessarily to those working there.

Businesses like restaurants, which depend on more than just good cooking and for whom the element of being 'in' or fashionable is so important, are particularly susceptible to the effects of adjustments in their feng-shui. Restaurant owners should try to ensure that the mouth of their main stove or oven faces either in the Direction of the owner's second best or *T'ien Yi* auspicious Direction (see pages 72-73).

FAVORABLE OFFICE DOOR AND DESK LOCATIONS

KUA NUMBER	*FU WEI* BEST DOOR DIRECTION	*SHENG CH'I* BEST DESK LOCATION
1	North	Southeast
2	Southwest	Northeast
3	East	South
4	Southeast	North
5 (if male)	Southwest	Northeast
5 (if female)	Northeast	Southwest
6	Northwest	West
7	West	Northwest
8	Northeast	Southwest
9	South	East

CREATING GOOD OFFICE FENG-SHUI

Unyielding rectangular furniture together with 'cutting' knife-like vertical blinds do not create a good feng-shui environment.

The same office which has been 'softened' with the addition of plants which help to absorb 'secret arrows' created by the angular furniture.

OFFICE LAYOUTS

This badly laid out office can be improved with minimal effort. Both the doorway and the window strike directly at the back of the office worker. Further 'secret arrows' are generated by the additional square table.

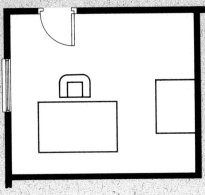

The chair is now pointed in an auspicious Direction and faces the doorway. *Ch'i* entering the room is soothed by the presence of a plant just inside the door. The additional table is now curved in such a way as to prevent the generation of 'secret arrows'.

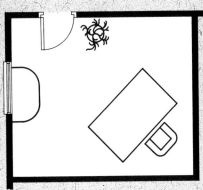

Protectors & Countermeasures

The essence of a good countermeasure is to treat the incoming 'secret arrows' by reflection, absorption or simply by blocking them. By reflecting 'secret arrows' you send them back to their source.

Having figured out where potential 'secret arrows' strike your home (see pages 14-15) now is the time to set up protectors and countermeasures. Protection of the front door is one of the main concerns of feng-shui, for it is through the main door that most of the *ch'i* enters the house.

The lion is a traditional guardian creature in Chinese temples where they are depicted in an almost mythological manner as they are no longer indigenous to China.

Protecting your front door

In Imperial China, the doors and gateways of palaces and temples were protected by stone lions. Nowadays many Chinese restaurants, even in London, are protected in this way. However, large stone or bronze lions are perhaps not easily accepted suburban front door ornaments.

If your front door has a 'secret arrow' aimed directly at it or is subject to cutting *ch'i* from the building opposite, then a painted Pa Kua symbol with a mirror at its centre, available in many Chinese supermarkets, can be used. More elaborate wooden tablets with the Pa Kua and guardian figures painted on them and made specifically to protect your door are an acceptable alternative.

The Pa Kua mirror

Be careful however in how you use a Pa Kua mirror. You will notice that the Trigrams on these Pa Kua mirrors are arranged in the Earlier Heaven Sequence (see page 35), unlike the Pa Kua we have used so far. When hanging it the *Ch'ien* Trigram (with three unbroken lines) should be at the top, although they are usually provided with a hanging hook.

The Pa Kua mirror is surprisingly potent and should never be used inside your home or aimed idly at a neighbour. The Pa Kua mirror is Yang and reflects *sha ch'i* back from where it comes from, whereas an ordinary mirror is Yin and attracts and passes on *ch'i*. Remember that these cures work and that in protecting your home they may correspondingly diminish the good feng-shui of the premises they are aimed at.

Using conventional mirrors

A full length mirror can also be used to disguise something such as a toilet door because by the rules of feng-shui, what you can't see can't affect you. You should however be careful with the placement of mirrors. Try

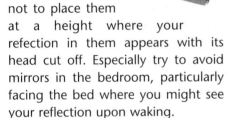

...he Pa Kua is enhanced by ...e presence of the door ...uardian god. This ...articular one should ...e placed on the ...ght-hand side ...f the door ...ooking ...wards).

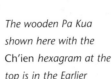

The wooden Pa Kua shown here with the Ch'ien hexagram at the top is in the Earlier Heaven Sequence.

not to place them at a height where your refection in them appears with its head cut off. Especially try to avoid mirrors in the bedroom, particularly facing the bed where you might see your reflection upon waking.

Mirrors can be used to enhance good qualities by apparently 'doubling them'. For example restaurants often use mirrors to double the apparent number of customers. In fact this technique was used very successfully in the opening of Michael Caine's latest restaurant in the USA.

Specifically, a mirror opposite the cash register represents the doubling of income. In the dining area a mirror will symbolize the doubling of the food on the table, and hence abundance for all the family.

Mirrors will also replace 'missing corners', where a section has been chopped out of an otherwise rectangular room.

Be careful however, that mirrors do not point directly out of the front door as they may reflect incoming beneficial *ch'i* away from the house. Many practitioners advise against using mirror tiles as these break up the image reflected in them and therefore harm the person or relationship reflected.

The Talisman of the Heavenly Messenger, representing the 28 constellations, is designed to seize and destroy spirits which can only move in straight lines.

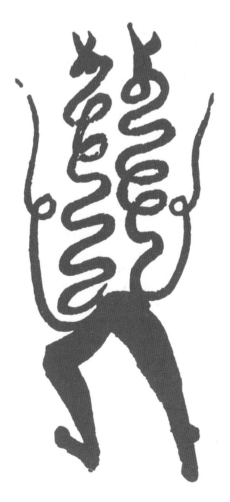

Sandy had his office on the Southeastern corner of a block of offices with a great view through curved picture windows overlooking a large intersection and along a straight street. His business was quite successful, but every now and then there would be a major reversal in fortune, an agent would fail to pay a very large bill or he would get entangled in complex and expensive legal cases. The result was that the business continued to make significant losses.

Sandy called in a feng-shui practitioner, who after a cursory look round the office pointed out an obelisk in the grounds of a disused church at the end of the street which pointed directly at Sandy's office. Sandy followed the feng-shui practitioner's recommendations and reluctantly had the curved windows curtained. He kept the curtains closed for the next five weeks, and was surprised to find that he was winning most of the new business he was pitching for.

A year later Sandy is a firm supporter of feng-shui methods and claims that he does not even miss the great view. The 'secret arrows' created by the obelisk are also deflected by a Pa Kua mirror which Sandy had fixed to the outside of his office window just to make sure.

Light, Plant & Water Enhancers & Cures

Cures and enhancers should be used to stimulate or suppress the feng-shui of a particular sector of a house, flat or even just a room, in each case using the Pa Kua to locate the correct sector.

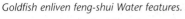
Goldfish enliven feng-shui Water features.

When you have decided on which sector to work on, then you need to decide exactly what sort of stimulation is required. The stimulation should take into account the Element of the sector. You can stimulate this by supplying an enhancer that 'creates' the Element required (see The Production Cycle, pages 36-37). The categories of enhancers or cures listed below and on pages 92-93 act to strengthen a particular sector or Element.

Light enhancers and cures

These bright reflective items include electric lights, candles or chandelier crystals which catch and transmute the sun's rays. Light is Yang in its action and stimulating. As light is universal it is not tied to one Element, but perhaps has a more specific affinity with Fire and is therefore particularly useful in the Southern quarter as well as the Earth

sectors of Northeast and Southwest (Fire creates Earth).

Although not recommended in traditional feng-shui texts, using lead crystal or cut glass to turn light coming through a window into a spectrum of colours, particularly where the room is dark, is an excellent way of introducing more Yang into and enlivening a room.

Mirrors reflect light as well but they are described in greater detail on pages 88-89 because they also deflect *sha ch'i* and are useful as protectors.

Plant enhancers and cures

Living plants and flowers help to soften otherwise hard Yang lines, but more importantly help to accumulate *ch'i*. As Wood they do well in the East or Southeastern sector which are attributed to Wood, or in the Southern quarter where Wood feeds Fire. Artificial but not

Left: This Chinese-made water feature could be used as a desk fountain in your office and will help to stimulate your career.

Right: Candles, statues and plants make for an environment conducive to accumulating beneficial ch'i.

dried (and therefore dead) imitations of plants and flowers are acceptable on a symbolic level, but are unlikely to generate as much beneficial *ch'i* as the real things.

Flowers, which lift the spirits under any conditions, also help to improve the feng-shui qualities of a room. Be careful not to keep them until they are dead, as dying, dead or dried flowers are too Yin and are not a desirable room feature. Prickly plants such as holly or cacti should also be avoided.

Water enhancers and cures

A fish tank or bowl containing koi or goldfish is just as effective as plants and flowers when dealing with a Water or Wood Direction. Goldfish of course are highly popular because of their colour, which is symbolic of happiness (red) and wealth (gold). Carp or koi were also a traditional temple pond fish.

There should be an odd number of fish, with 9 suggested as an ideal number. An odd number of fish is always recommended, with a black fish included to help absorb any negative energies. Do however consider the colour of the fish carefully, as red fish for example may introduce some element of Fire. Black fish will symbolize Water.

Small fountains are great stimulators of Water and will also help create Wood (because of the Production Cycle of the Elements). Fountains are an apt feng-shui symbol by virtue of their passing water through air. Be careful however not to introduce a fountain so large that it swamps an area either physically or from a feng-shui point of view.

Wind & Earth
Enhancers & Cures

Appropriate combinations of or extensions to the list below and on pages 90-91 are only limited by your imagination. Think it through carefully, but if you find you have overstimulated a sector, you can always dismantle your enhancer. Try it for yourself and may your luck increase.

Rocks often have personalities, so be certain that their form does not suggest anything malevolent or threatening.

The categories of enhancers or cures listed below and on pages 90-91 act to strengthen a particular sector or Element.

Wind enhancers and cures

Objects which symbolize wind or are wind instruments relate closely to *feng*. A classic cure is the wind-chime because it produces tinkling sounds at the slightest breeze. It is essential that the pipes are hollow. Wooden wind-chimes are preferable, but hollow metal ones are good in areas where they would enhance either Metal or the Element that Metal creates, Water. Wind-chimes hung in the Western sector of your home will help your children's luck, whilst stimulating the opposite sector in the East will increase family cohesion. Stimulating the Southwestern sector improves your relationship potential and may also attract suitable partners for your offspring.

Bamboo flutes, which have a symbolic as well as a *feng* association, are good if used in pairs and hung at an angle to remove the threat of *sha*

ch'i from overhead beams. Bells can also be included here. Owl tail feathers were often also used in temples to symbolically represent *feng*.

Movement enhancers and cures

Flags, silk banners, mobiles, windmills and fans all help to stimulate *ch'i* flow and circulate *feng*. The principle is to provide even the gentlest breeze to prevent congesting or stagnating *ch'i*. In an airless room these 'cures' may be less successful. Modern feng-shui practitioners consider that TVs, stereos and videos fall into the category of moving *ch'i* stimulators.

Colour enhancers and cures

Colour serves to balance the Yin and Yang elements in a room or house. These beneficial qualities are covered in an earlier chapter (see pages 64-65).

Earth enhancers and cures

Statues and ornamental stones are used to redress the Yin-Yang balance in gardens by adding extra Yang. This is evident in Chinese or Japanese gardens where the weight of a good smooth rock can often 'anchor' and balance the rest of the garden. Their placement however must be carefully thought out.

Magical enhancers and cures

Other traditional 'cures' include door guardians and talismans written in Chinese 'grass' script in red or black ink by a Taoist priest on a peachwood tablet. Because of the complexity of these and the need to be able to write a special sort of Chinese script, these are best left to the experts.

Light is an important Yang constituent in a room. By breaking up white light and dispersing it through natural crystals, the resultant rainbow stimulates and uplifts the ch'i. Natural crystals are preferable for achieving this aim.

NEED SOME HELP?

WHEN TO ASK FOR PROFESSIONAL HELP

Feng-shui has the advantage that once the basic principles of *ch'i*, the five Elements and the Pa Kua are firmly understood, there is much you can do to enhance your own feng-shui. I do however caution you strongly against 'doing the feng-shui' for friends. It is not fair to them and may involve you in taking on karmic responsibilities for messing about with their luck.

If in doubt, or if the situation seems desperate, then do seek out a proper feng-shui *hsein-sheng* or master. These individuals are not easy to find and since the rise in

popularity of feng-shui, increasingly well-intentioned amateurs are offering their services. In the UK the Feng Shui Society can point you in the direction of a reputable practitioner. In other countries it is

best to ask for a written diagnosis in English. You should then consider the diagnosis in the light of what you have learnt in this book before making any radical changes. It is usually not necessary to make major alterations and the use of the countermeasures and enhancers discussed over the last six pages will often do the trick.

You should always agree a fee up front, before the feng-shui practitioner begins his work. If the practitioner asks for additional money for 'blessings' or 'prayers' or counsels wholesale architectual changes, then perhaps you should treat the advice with a large grain of salt.

風水 FENG-SHUI

GLOSSARY

cardinal points	North, South, East, West
ch'i	the vital energy of the universe, or 'cosmic breath'
compass school	the Fukien school of feng-shui which uses the feng-shui compass to diagnose *ch'i* flows. Early master was Wang Chih (circa 960 AD)
Direction	one of the 24 compass Directions, such as *tzu* in the North
earlier heaven sequence	a circular arrangement of the 8 Trigrams such that the Trigram *Ch'ien* is in the South. Used on defensive pa kua and for burial site feng-shui
Elements	the five Chinese Elements: Water, Fire, Wood, Earth, Metal
fang-shih	master of Taoist magic
feng	wind
feng sha	a noxious *ch'i* destroying wind
feng-shui	the Chinese system of maximising the accumulation of *ch'i* to improve the quality of life, literally 'wind and water'
feng-shui hsien-sheng	a practitioner of feng-shui
form school	feng-shui practice common in Kiangsi which uses the form of the surrounding landscape to determine the location of the *ch'i* flow
geomancy	a European and African form of earth-divining totally unrelated to feng-shui. The early missionaries in China in the 1870s incorrectly used 'geomancy' as a translation of feng-shui
hexagram	the 64 figures formed by placing one Trigram on top of another. A figure with eight lines, either broken or unbroken
hsing	one of the five Chinese Elements, Water, Fire, Wood, Earth, Metal
hsiu	constellations
I Ching	the Chinese *Classic of Changes*, a philosophical and divinatory book based on the 64 hexagrams
intercardinal points	Northeast, Northwest, Southeast, Southwest
kua	see Trigram (*kua* in Chinese)
later heaven sequence	a circular arrangement of the 8 Trigrams such that the Trigram *Li* is in the South. Used for feng-shui of houses and cities
lo p'an	the feng-shui compass
lo shu	the magic square with 9 chambers, whose numbers add up to 15 in any direction, connected with the Later Heaven Sequence of Trigrams
pa kua	the eight-sided or circular arrangement of the eight Trigrams
'secret arrow'	a *ch'i*-destroying alignment of an adjacent road, property, etc.
sector	one of the cardinal or intercardinal points, ie North, South, East, West, Northeast, Northwest, Southeast, Southwest
sha or *sha ch'i*	stagnant *ch'i*
shui	water
t'ai-chi	the great Absolute from which everything else came
Taoism	a Chinese religious and mystical belief concerned with Tao and the way of flow and harmony
t'ien	heaven
Trigram	eight figures made up of three Yang (whole) or Yin (broken) lines
tzu	due North (and other meanings)
Yang	male active energy, the opposite of Yin
Yang Yun-Sung	early master of the Form School of feng-shui (circa 888 AD)
Yin	female passive energy, the opposite of Yang

FURTHER READING

Chuen, Lam Kam   *The Feng Shui Handbook*
Gaia Books, London, 1995

Eitel, Ernest   *Feng-shui: or the Rudiment of Natural Science in China*
Cokaygne, Cambridge, 1973

Lip, Evelyn   *Chinese Geomancy*
Times Books International, Singapore, 1979

Rossbach, Sarah   *Interior Design with Feng-shui*
Rider, London, 1987

Skinner, Stephen   *Feng Shui, the Practitioner's Manual*
London, 1998

Skinner, Stephen   *Living Earth Manual of Feng-Shui*
Penguin, London, 1989*

Too, Lillian   *Applied Pa-Kua and Lo Shu Feng Shui*
Konsep, Kuala Lumpur, 1993

Too, Lillian   *Chinese Numerology in Feng Shui*
Konsep Books, Kuala Lumpur, 1994

Too, Lillian   *The Complete Illustrated Guide to Feng Shui*
Element, Shaftesbury, 1996*

Too, Lillian   *Feng Shui*
Konsep Books, Kuala Lumpur, 1993

Too, Lillian   *Practical Applications of Feng Shui*
Konsep Books, Kuala Lumpur, 1994

Walters, Derek   *Feng Shui Handbook: A Practical Guide to Chinese Geomancy and Environmental Harmony*
Aquarian Press, London, 1991*

Wong, Eva   *Feng-Shui: The Ancient Wisdom of Harmonious Living for Modern Times*
Shambhala, London, 1996*

Feng-shui Magazine   Available from Affinity Publishing, 2nd Floor, 1-5 Clerkenwell Rd, London, EC1M 5PA

* these books form a thorough and balanced introduction to feng-shui

FENG-SHUI

INDEX